Until the Red Swallows It All

Praise for *Until the Red Swallows It All*

"The LA streets had their Bukowski, and the southern border deserts had their Bowden, and now the red dirt plains and blackjack hills of Oklahoma have their Parker. The fierce, urgent language in *Until The Red Swallows It All* never lets us forget what has been lost, or what might have been, even as it tells a survivor's tale. Post-lament, pre-celebration, real-time warning: this book might break your mind and open your heart."

Phil Condon, author of *River Street*

"Mason Parker has a heart. It floods with the rain, cracks with the wildfires, and glows with the bioluminescence of a mid-summer firefly. If you've ever given a shit about anything with the wholeness of your very being, this book is for you. If you haven't, hopefully this book will help."

Shy Watson, author of *Horror Vacui*

"Mason Parker's is a strong fresh voice grown right out of Oklahoma and into Montana, via many other landscapes along the way. How he weds the erotics of geography with his own struggling sensuality recalls the candor of T. T. Williams, but is entirely his own. A fine describer of place, event, and the lives of his own and other species, Parker dives deep into happenstance and personal history and comes up with a plum of a book. Twining boyhood ritual with a young man's regrets and joys, he arrives at a sharp sense of the Now — a time when fierce objection to our environmental catastrophe requires equally fierce celebration of what remains, in spite of us. Parker manages both, with grace."

**Robert Michael Pyle,
author of *The Thunder Tree***

"Mason Parker has given us the rarest of gifts: a book that is true, a straight shot distilled from the grit and tears of the broken heart land. Summon the unflinching courage to match his. Read this to know what ails us."

Richard Manning, author of *If It Sounds Good, It Is Good: Seeking Subversion, Transcendence and Solace In America's Music*

"*Until the Red Swallows It All* surprised me. There is no sentimentalism in Parker's writing, just descriptions of a world that so many of us know and hope to never forget. The wheel keeps turning, with the same dilemmas and celebrations. Parker's patience for the craft is astounding."

Noah Cicero, author of *Bipolar Cowboy*

"Mason Parker writes with voice, vigor, and a keen attention to the natural world and the creatures, including us humans, that haunt it. These essays are funny, poignant and dark, all with a deeply rooted sense of place. A good ride."

Bart Schaneman, author of *The Silence is the Noise*

Until the Red Swallows It All

by *Mason Parker*

Trident Press
Boulder, CO

ISBN: 978-1-951226-14-5

Cover art and design by Rachel Pfeffer

Published by Trident Press
940 Pearl St.
Boulder, CO 80302

tridentcafe.com/trident-press-titles

"The Generations Forget Each Other" originally appeared in *A Beautiful Resistance 5: After Empire*.

For the roadkill.

Geography, for example, deals with the determinant action of general natural forces, such as soil composition or climatic conditions, on the economic structures of a society, and thus on the corresponding conception that such a society can have of the world. Psychogeography could set for itself the study of the precise laws and specific effects of the geographical environment, whether consciously organized or not, on the emotions and behavior of individuals.

—Guy Debord, *Introduction to a Critique of Urban Geography* (1955)

We can expect human egos to be pockmarked with the traces of hyperobjects. We are all burnt by ultraviolet rays. We all contain water in about the same ratio as Earth does, and salt water in the same ratio that the oceans do. We are poems about the hyperobject Earth.

—Timothy Morton, *Hyperobjects: Philosophy and Ecology After the End of the World* (2013)

I couldn't unpeach the peaches.

—Annie Dillard, *A Pilgrim at Tinker Creek* (1974)

CONTENTS

POOLS

They say Tenkiller Lake was named for the ten men who died building the dam, ten bodies pummeled and trapped in concrete while the dam ages and cracks, but they do not. That's a lie. The lake was named for a Cherokee family that operated the ferry when the Illinois River was still untamed. I've always liked the way it rolls off the tongue. Ten-kill-er, where the cliffs rise from the shore like decomposing ribs. I gripped hickories and skirted the bluff, leapt from the edge and sensed a weightlessness merging with the wind as gravity pushed me down into the water. There are no natural lakes in Oklahoma, only pools that exist through a network of machinery—dams and pipes that run for miles.

On the southern plains, we swim in pools that dissolve the boundaries of self. You open your eyes underwater and time slows down. It creeps over your skin. Sound bounces through your head to end up nowhere. We swim in pools of viscous oil. We come to be in the darkness of that oil. Gestate there like the wet grubs we stick on our hooks to bait striper as we float lazily down the Illinois. I would twist my line in a fisherman's knot, fastening down colorful lures or hooks baited with stinky brown putty to draw out the channel catfish. Cousin Charlie noodled. Cig in mouth, bait in hand. He shoved his fist into a hole and prayed he didn't catch a snapping turtle instead. On summer days, when the blistering sun struck the water unabated, bow fishermen speared alligator gar as they surfaced through the rush of the Illinois, putting an arrow through their long bodies and letting them drift downriver splitting swells, spinning lifeless among the eddies. The dead fish drifted beside chicken shit and guts, pumped by Tyson into the river in exchange for campaign contributions to Oklahoma's Attorney General and future head of the EPA, Scott Pruitt.

I grew up in a big house amid a forest of post and blackjack oak where the borderlands of the Cross Timbers collide with the Great Plains a few miles to the west. Our home was positioned on the curve of a U-shaped neighborhood with two cul-de-sacs. In late autumn, the trees stood gnarled and strong like a sea of metallic prosthetics hugging the curves of the planet and pinching the vast expanse of blue sky that came down to meet them.

It was overseen by a homeowner's association and a hierarchy of housewives. They had clear cut a refuge and built an echo chamber. It worked pretty well until they got tired of hearing their own voices.

In the back yards, there were always pools.

Beyond the forest, AWACs lifted from the runways of the Air Force base, gliding and wobbling through the sky—big planes with saucer shaped radars mounted on the fuselage. As a child, I imagined them soaring over the deserts of Iraq, fighting for the right side in the War on Terror. The government stole poor folk's land and expanded the Air Force base. They called that eminent domain. There is not much left of the forest anymore. Oklahoma City encroached and chewed up most of the oaks and dogwoods.

Between the cul-de-sacs was a hole. They filled that hole with water and called it a pond. As the summer day's last light spread across our shoulders, we waded into the turbid water, everything moving around us in chaotic harmony. There were more horny toads and fireflies then. We trapped them not knowing any better, not knowing as kids that our lives would be defined by the planet's impermanence. We know that well enough now. It's been years since I've seen a horny toad skittering across my parents' land, and the fireflies that once lit up the night sky like a great big irradiated blanket now rarely poke through the dark in dazzling little pinpricks. We caught them and squeezed their bioluminescent ass goop onto our cheeks, sending our howls echoing across the flatness of the plains.

Mike Connor from the brown house on the south side of the cul-de-sac used to pay us to kill copperheads.

"I'll give you boys a Washington for every snake you bring me."

"Cool, a dollar!"

"Not a dollar, kid, a quarter. I've got to keep Susie safe!" he said, stroking his Yorkie as she snarled with her eyes locked on our throats.

We trudged into the thick of the cattails, cargo pockets rattling with containers of silver pellets, because every kid knew that silver pellets were deadlier than copper BBs—a child's hollow tip. The wind blew through the tall grass along the shore, so it swayed this way and that. The muddy water sparkled. Frogs and snapping turtles splashed into the pond, leaving ripples along our warpath. A hillbilly disco.

When we happened upon a snake, we jumped and screamed "oh shit!" as they slithered away unscathed. We weren't much good at killing copperheads, never made a Washington. All the fertilizer and insecticide that was washed into the pond thinned their ranks more than we ever did, but we fancied ourselves killers. Killers like the ranchers whose rattlesnake roundups collect half a million skins every year to keep them from harming the cattle or the kids.

One night in August, after a summer rain, we grilled hamburgers on the patio amid the June bugs—thick, buzzing, and dumb—colliding with the glass door that led into my parents' living room. Uncle Tim said, "There's this new type of rattlesnake that doesn't rattle. Y'all heard of this?"

"Is that right?" I said.

"Sure is. They got a huge rattlesnake roundup right here in Oklahoma. It's like a carnival. Ferris wheels and funnel cakes and skee ball and shit," he said.

"I think I've heard of that," I said.

"Bet you have. One of the biggest in the world. They keep killing hundreds of thousands of snakes every year and all that's left is these quiet ones."

"Creepy."

"You said it. Now these quiet little bastards keep reproducing and their offspring come out with the same mutation. No rattler, just empty skin. It's crinkled and hangs there like this—" Uncle Tim crooked his finger in front of his face and wiggled it around.

But we didn't see any rattlesnakes near the pond. Most of the splashing and stirring came from bullfrogs taking flight in startling leaps, arms and legs flailing in defiance at the weight of the sky. The frogs sometimes fell victim to a lawnmower or a weed-wacker. They sliced them up and sent their remains tumbling across the green grass, entrails hanging from their stomachs in wet velvet banners. We froze the carcasses so my cousins could fry their legs on the Fourth of July. They were always stingy about who got to eat them.

A flock of Canadian geese settled in the neighborhood. They loved that dirty old pond. Everyone was fond of those plump, waddling birds until the streets got caked in goose shit, and it was impossible to walk your dog without dragging them along as they licked the concrete, lapping up the sun-dried feces. That flock still lives in the neighborhood because no one has come up with a good way to get rid of them. But they are not enjoyed; they are tolerated.

Someone hit a stray dog in the cul-de-sac by the pond and left it there. The neighborhood kids gathered around transfixed as it began to rot. It was hard to tell, but it must have been some sort of shepherd mix, and the fur around its mouth had a distinguished gray color to it. It wasn't a young dog. Maggots and crows picked at it as the heat baked its flesh and fluids into the cement. I wanted to move the poor thing somewhere where the earth could take it, but animal control came and peeled it up. There was a stain left there for months.

The neighborhood was separated into one-acre plots, and for a while the lot behind our house was uncleared and undeveloped, a tangled web of wild abutting our meticulously kept lawn. The neighborhood kids crawled through the large oaks, swinging from the vines hanging between the limbs, and we often got lost in that little patch of forest. Surrounded by empty lots of excavated red dirt and new homes, it stood apart looking pristine and resilient. As we crawled through the undergrowth, unseen things moved in the vegetation, sending my mind to the jungles of Brazil or the Congo, while thorns from wild roses poked through the skin of my shins and calves. The punctures went untreated until late in the day when we emerged on the other side and the sky reappeared above the flat stretch of the southern horizon. I made my way back to the house, only then noticing the blood that ran from the cuts on my legs, streaming down, and staining the tops of my white cotton socks.

In the living room, there was a set of overstuffed couches covered with floral patterns and a glass top coffee table held up by plaster statues of ornamental elephants. When the dog's face itched he scratched it on their tusks. He scratched himself over and over until the tusks broke off and fell from the elephant's face into the shaggy white tufts of the sheepskin rug below. My dad superglued them on, but the dog scratched and scratched until they came off again. At some point, he gave up and the elephants were left without their tusks like they had been poached for ivory.

I cleaned myself up on that red and brown, floral patterned couch, feet propped on the glass table. Hovering above me, my mom picked deer ticks from my head. It was a soothing feeling when she ran her fingers through my hair, as if my head might float from my shoulders and become a quiet star, out of sight.

A row of blackjack oaks lined the west side of our lot. One tree split as it rose from the ground, forming two trunks that could be climbed into the canopy. The leaves of a blackjack are shaped like bloated little phoenixes bursting from the cluster of acorns, and one day I found a toucan perched among them. I knew exactly how that tropical bird ended up on the American prairie. Up the road was a mansion with peacocks and horses and swans behind a fence of red brick and wrought iron. It belonged to a millionaire who won the lottery in California and moved to flyover country for the cheap cost of living. He bought up real estate and became a slumlord. He was busted pimping young girls out of his massage parlor where all the rooms had different themes. One was a jungle. One was a beach. One was a Japanese bath house. I ate huevos rancheros at the diner across the way and watched the girls come and go. Their skin was tanned and hardened, and they were always laughing.

The mansion burned down twice. Some whispered of insurance fraud. I wonder what happened to all those peacocks. Those horses. Those swans. The fence around the mansion still holds stone lions that sit proudly with their chests puffed out looking over the road into the flat expanse pushing towards America's borders in every direction, continuing to guard an empty home.

SOMEDAY, I'LL SEE
THE WORLD IN YOU

————————————

Some years after Grandpa Bryson died I sat at the dinner table drinking iced tea with my aunts and Grandma O'Hare. Grandma brewed tea in her coffee maker, so it always tasted smoky like Hills Brothers. They gossiped as I stared through the window at the finches splashing around the bath in the garden. Their beaks and black eyes looked like they were stuck on as an afterthought.

Grandma said to me, "You know your Grandpa Bryson's parents were first cousins."

"No... I didn't know that..."

I looked around the table at my aunts who were staring into the brown haze of their iced tea. I imagine they already knew this, but I'd just reached the age where I could be brought in on the family secrets, those that were deemed inappropriate for a kid. The façade of functionality cracks, the truth comes out, and your family becomes far more interesting than it ever was before.

"You don't know that, Mom," said Aunt Doris.

"Sure I do. Bobby Sue and Frank Bryson were first cousins. Makes sense. I always thought Vandal might have been mentally defective," Grandma said tapping the side of her head with her index finger.

"Mom!" my aunts howled.

"I don't think you should say that, Grandma."

"Well, why the hell not? I got the right to say whatever I want about that man. I was married to the son of a bitch for years. Old inbred redneck."

My grandma is the uncontested matriarch of the family. She's a kind and affectionate woman, and I always thought there was room in her heart for the whole world. She just reserved the most contemptuous corners for Grandpa Bryson.

"Well you married him!" Aunt Darlene pointed out.

"You think I don't know that, Darlene? He was the worst of the five!" said Grandma.

"I believe it. Y'all remember those Bryson family reunions? There were more people than there were teeth!"

There is a reason for the poor dental hygiene that characterizes the Bryson family. For the past century or so, they've been perfecting the craft of distilling jet-fuel-strong corn liquor deep in the woods of southeast Oklahoma. They began running moonshine into Arkansas during the prohibition era when Al Capone and Lucky Luciano set up shop in Hot Springs, AR and Oklahoma was still Indian Territory. Over time, they took to drinking it. Family lore says they guzzled so much of that stuff it burned the teeth right out of their heads. Now they are known for their gummy smiles and indecipherable dialect. A rag-tag band, feral and at home in the backwoods.

My biological Grandfather's name was Vandal. My Grandma O'Hare remarried the same year my folks got hitched and her husband, Lloyd, had always been my grandfather for all intents and purposes. But biologically it was Vandal Bryson. They tell me Grandpa Bryson inherited some of those drinking habits though he didn't make the stuff himself. He drank from a two liter every day—one liter of cheap whiskey and one liter of Coke. He got real nasty with my uncles, Jim and Bill, and made them fist fight as he sucked down that hooch, spectating in a drunken delirium.

"He was a mean old hillbilly. He'd drink all day. Make us

beat up on each other just so he could watch." That's what Uncle Jim says.

But I remembered a different man. A broken man. He had a round nose and a shiny head he hid under a navy-blue hat with tufts of disheveled hair that stuck out from the sides. He was an old man who finished every phone call with the same question, "Is your soul still on fire for the Lord?" while his wife Martha breathed heavily on the other end of the line, thinking we didn't know she was listening to every word.

I'd say, "Yes, Grandpa." Even when that fire turned into a blazing void inside me, hungry for meaning and moral certitude. If I were honest, I would've said, "Is my soul still on fire? Yes. It's a great big fire. A wildfire even. Chaotic, destructive, unpredictable. Oh yeah Grandpa my soul is on fire. But for the Lord? No, not for the Lord."

But I stuck to the script. "Yes Grandpa, my soul is on fire for the Lord. Absolutely."

Then he'd say, "When are we going fishing, bud?"

"Whenever you want, Grandpa."

Occasionally he followed through with it.

One morning, when the day's temperature was set to be 110 degrees, he pulled up in his old single-cab Mazda pickup. The leather covering the bench seat was worn out, so there was only white webbing and yellow foam. The body was flat black with a coat of primer. As he rolled into the driveway, a mist of evaporating antifreeze rose from the engine. In the bed were two beat up old Rhino rods and a brown tackle box whose cracks were covered with duct tape. "Bryson" was scrawled in sharpie across the top. There were half a dozen jugs filled with water. I didn't know it then, but this was going to be our last fishing trip.

This old man and I rumbled through the farmlands. The sky was far reaching. It bounced between my senses and a pale expanse, becoming a nebulous vastness that consumed itself endlessly. To my left was the shadow of a monster spread out behind the steering wheel with a calloused hand on the stick shift. His mind was only half clinging to his senses. I could see that. I stared at him as he focused on the road. The pieces of a broken spirit were jostling around, barely held together by the glue of Jesus Christ. That was his best shot at redemption. His children had all but disavowed him, so Jesus would have to do.

When I try to understand the origins of his maliciousness, I imagine a child that came to be inside the ruthless fog of poverty. A dirty little kid drudging through the foothills of the Kiamichis. In the fall, the rolling hills changed colors, yellows and oranges and reds, in kaleidoscopic waves that breached the sky. It's a place where folks went missing because they stumbled onto the wrong marijuana farm, and, for a cut, the local sheriff looked the other way. This child was a part of the land like those hills, rising and falling, lumbering through the green grass and the dead leaves and the gusting wind that could blow a kid right from his feet.

There can be a certain curdled sense of self defined by Oklahoma. Age sets in and all you can see is nothingness in every direction. It wears at the edges of your soul. He looked down into a gorge filled with all his conceivable selves only to see a million piles of bones covered with anger and loss. As he faced his final years, he hoped to drift into the afterlife with some peace of mind, but the people he abused just wouldn't give it to him.

I use my relationship with my Grandpa as a proxy for coping with the reality of ecocide. Like the narrative we stretch over planetary collapse, his story is characterized by invisible tragedies. A cathedral of moving pieces, material and immaterial, arises from the mythology of dark forests and dangerous backwaters. Sanctuaries of the animalistic. My relationship to him was one of perpetual loss. Every time I thought I had him figured out, he shapeshifted or wrestled free like a crazed coyote. Extinction, climate change, deforestation, they too resist my attempts to grasp them fully.

For work, Grandpa Bryson drove a big purple dump

truck. When he picked me up we'd spend the afternoon riding around town. We always stopped at a polo field on the north side of Oklahoma City where a smiling Mexican man dumped a Bobcat full of horse shit in the bed and gave us a thumbs up. We carried the load to wheat farms where they used it to fertilize their crops. I shoveled and sprayed the bed down when we finished. Shoveling all that shit was grounding, visceral, and I enjoyed it.

On the road, he tried to pry information from me. He asked what the family thought of him. I told him they didn't say much about him at all.

Other times, I stayed in his creaky old lake house with striped bass mounted on the walls. At dawn, we went to his favorite spot on the banks of the Arkansas and collected bait. We flipped over rocks and giant earthworms wriggled around in the mud, exposed to the damp air and the light of morning. We spent an hour filling little Styrofoam cups until they were writhing and overflowing with worms. I was covered in dirt for the rest of the day. All this time Grandpa Bryson cracked jokes, speaking from his chest rather than his mouth, and releasing high-flying laughs that came from somewhere deep inside.

He always felt like an extension of the landscape, existing through the dirt and the dung and the rocks and the water. There is a reason why they call people like Vandal Bryson hillbillies. You can't have a hillbilly without the hills. They are a reflection of the place they came to be.

But the old man that I knew in those days wasn't the same one sitting next to me in the truck that day. For the first time, the signs of dementia were setting in. Those signs turned into midnight visits to the nursing home to settle him down because he was roaming the halls naked, yelling incoherent demands, and making passes at fed-up nurses.

The wheat leaned to the west, and heat rose from the asphalt, distorting the road ahead. The sky lifted itself from the ground with casual breaths, like the clouds were doing push-ups on invisible arms. We were lost. The man next to me had a shadow cast across his brain that left our destination in the dark. It hid his moments and his memories in a deteriorating panoramic picture, a snapshot of a life he'd already lived.

We had driven around aimlessly for an hour and a half. He couldn't afford to keep buying antifreeze to fill up his leaky radiator, but he also couldn't afford to fix his radiator. That's why he kept all those one-gallon jugs in the back of the truck. We stopped every thirty minutes to fill the thing up. It hissed and sizzled as we opened the hood. We stuck the funnel in and slowly poured the water. The jugs burned my hand from sitting in the sun all morning.

As we looked at the grease-covered engine he said, "I'm not sure I know where we're at. Thought the turn was back there a couple of miles ago. I'm not remembering things as well as I used to."

"Well, that's alright. We can keep looking. We'll find it eventually."

I was wrong. The day pushed on and the heat came in more and more fierce. We drove and we drove. We stopped at every gas station until there were no more gas stations. We turned down a gravel road.

"Maybe this is it. I think this is it."

His voice sounded stretched and desperate.

At the end of the road was an old trailer. Scattered around the yard were little indications of someone's life, their hobbies and habits. A target filled with holes from a .22, a chicken coop, a rusted-out Nova, a kiddie pool. Thick elms rose up, shading the trailer from the relentless sun.

"You wait here, bud. I'm gonna go in and see if they have a phone."

Ten minutes later a thin man with long hair and a tank top emerged from the trailer. He was holding three frozen water bottles and a clunky Nokia cell phone. He trudged across grass and dirt and mulch, weaving through lawnmowers and basketball hoops, a long cigarette hanging from his mouth.

"How's it going, boy? Your grandpa tells me you're lost. Hot day not to be knowing where you're going, don't you think?"

"Yeah, I was thinking he knew."

He laughed.

"That man there has got no idea where he's going. Hell, he doesn't know where he's at. Anyway, I got y'all a couple waters here. They're frozen so they should last you a while. He's inside trying to get hold of somebody on the landline, but I don't think it's working. He told me there was a kid out here. With this heat and all, I figured I'd come out and make sure everything was good. See if you might have more luck getting hold of somebody than he's had."

"Thanks. I appreciate that. And the water."

"Sure thing."

He pulled a long drag off his Marlboro.

"Well, guess I'll go back in, see if they made any progress. Bring the phone in when you're done."

I sat there trying to get through to my aunt on that old Nokia. The phone rang irregularly, cutting in and out. Reception was bad. She answered, but I could only hear bits and pieces, and she could only hear enough to incite a wave of panic. I imagine she heard "We are lost. We are at a trailer in the woods."

The screen door swung open and Grandpa Bryson walked out. He waved a lazy hand as a gesture of thanks and goodbye. He got back in the truck and pulled a can of Grizzly from his back pocket. He shoved a big horseshoe into his lower lip and extended the can out to me.

"I'm ok, thanks."

He chuckled. "That's what I was hoping you'd say... Well, I still don't know where we're going. I hate to say it, but there might not be any fishing today."

I returned the phone, and we got back on the road.

As the sun set, the sky, always the sky, over the vast fields of wheat, above the monocrop eating the horizon and the biodiversity, blazed in a red that consumed the clouds and obscured the bouncing oil rigs cracking the endless flat. The wheat became illuminated like the open mouth of heaven. The tyranny of all that open space melted into a sensuous ensemble. I began to feel its complexity shaking my bones, each stroke painting my perception. The ones that go unnoticed through the rigmarole of our daily grind. Then the truck began to putter and the engine sounded like it was going to explode, so Grandpa Bryson pulled to the side of the road and we were once again bent over the engine compartment until he finally remembered that he needed to refill the radiator from one of those gallon jugs that had been sliding around in the bed of the truck since we left. And I wondered how it took him so long to remember that.

He never existed in my life as a person, only as an enigma. I was born of him but into his shadow. He was chaos. A collection of stories and myths spread over flesh and bone. I saw him as a wave rising from the landscape of Oklahoma, in part because my relationship to both is defined by precariousness. It's an intimate, material relation to someone and something that I can't discern. An eternal connection that pushes through time in ways seen and unseen. Like my grandfather, the planet that we've been told exists is no more. It is being shaped and reshaped by climate change and deforestation and extinction and drought and Indigenous genocide and civilizational collapse.

"Is your soul still on fire?"

"Yes, my soul is on fire."

We turned the truck into a dusty gas station. A woman in a worn out Tweety Bird shirt with a mole over her drawn-on eyebrow told us to make a left out of the parking lot and keep driving for three miles. Around that time, we should see an on ramp. If we took 240 West, we'd be heading in the right direction to get us home.

We pulled up to my Grandma O'Hare's house. You could tell everybody had been sitting in the kitchen staring out the window past the finches waiting for that rickety Mazda to pull up in a haze of radiator mist. After our phone call, Aunt Darlene must have sent out a distress signal. The whole family was standing at the bottom of the driveway glaring up toward the truck, through the windshield into Grandpa Bryson's senseless eyes.

"You think I should go say hi?" Grandpa Bryson asked.

"Maybe next time."

I don't know if a person can ever get forgiveness once they've done something truly wrong. Why should they? The people they damage have got to live with that shit for the rest of their lives. People go looking for redemption, good people and bad people. We've been told that we can be forgiven if we want to be. But Grandpa Bryson's bad decisions are still stuck in time. Mistakes like ice cubes in the freezer. I think he'd have done just about anything to see them melt away. Some part of him really believed that was possible, but it just wasn't.

His wife left him lying on the floor the night he fell. That's how it goes with old folks, right? There's a fall from which they never recover. Well that's what happened, and Martha decided she'd take care of it in the morning. Grandma thought that was his comeuppance for leaving her lying in the tub once when she was pregnant. She finished her bath and couldn't get up. He was drunk and thought it was funny, her swollen and rolling around like that. So she saw it as the universe getting back at the bastard one more time before he kicked it.

His last year was spent wasting away in an old folks home on the Southside. There were manic episodes punctuated by moments of clarity. His eyes bouncing around the room propelled by an empty confusion. Then one day he died.

He was laid there in the casket with the uncanny look of a dead family member and none of the waving aloofness that rooted his character to the land. The wild gray hair that stuck out from the sides of his head was neatly combed behind his ears. He wore a fine-fitting suit and some sort of makeup was smeared across his cheeks. No one seemed bothered by any of it. There was this box of tissue that everyone just kept passing along. No one ever took one.

I imagine everybody had their own reasons why they weren't struck by a particularly strong sense of loss. Many people were happy to be rid of him. As for me, I didn't know what I was losing or how to process the loss of something I didn't understand. There was sadness, a sense of melancholy. But loss? No.

Grandpa Bryson's blood and those memories that connected him to the hills, they run through me like fire. I was left with a way of existing pulled from the mythology I forged to explain my grandfather's cruelty. Over time, there arose an understanding of how to process grief for something that transcended my scope of being, my finite perception. Each role he plays in my mind, the feral child, the abusive drunk, the bass-wrangling churchgoer, and the shell cracked with senility, is a puzzle piece to be put together in a fog. The real cost was hidden. It wasn't the loss of what was, but what could have been.

On the way home, I sank into the backseat of my mom's car, looking out of the tinted window across a field. I saw something I hadn't seen before. It rose from the plains, looking more like a launch pad for a spacecraft than an oil rig. Something from outer space. A fracking rig. Below it, miles of pipes and spikes and proppants were seething with chemical cocktails. A hundred different pieces held together by black gunk and greed. Invisible things.

DEEP-INJECTION WELLS

Grandma and Grandad Owens lived on five acres wooded with oaks and blanketed with ryegrass that rose to my waist, brimming with grasshoppers that buzzed in startled spasms followed by flights toward the cloudless sky. Insectoid angels fallen from heaven. It felt like paradise walking among those cursed, earth-bound things. A long gravel driveway snaked from the top of the hill, through the five acres to the mailbox. Grandad drove his pickup down in the morning, pulling a pack of Winstons from beneath his hat where he hid them from Grandma.

Then the wind came and blew it all away.

The sky fell on a May afternoon, and their home disappeared into the darkness of a tornado that left only the oaken bones to sop up the humidity after the swirling blackness went east. It took the trees and the ryegrass with it. I imagine those grasshoppers were the closest to heaven they'd ever get. In the years to come, the rye grass grew back but the crooked, grayed oaks never did. That lot is still empty except for an old double wide that my cousin Charlie lives in. The walls got torn out and some thieves kicked in the doors a couple times wearing Carhartt beanies and red bandanas, ransacking the place with the bungling agility and persistence only those on an amphetamine binge can muster. They copped a flat screen and a Mossberg 12-gauge. There is an empty horse corral that my uncle built for a woman who came to live with him two decades ago. She drove up from Baton Rouge but decided Oklahoma didn't suit her. My uncle doesn't talk about it much. Part of the fence blew over on a windy afternoon, and nobody had any reason to fix it.

The houses on either side of that five acres were left untouched, but their lawns were littered with the anatomy of my grandparents' home: drywall, floor tiles, and insulation. Lumber mingled with sharp, rusted nails atop a layer of compacted dirt. Everything disappeared from the inside, the furniture and knick-knacks lifted and taken away. That's what bothered Grandma Owens most. She lost her photo albums and the family bible.

Someone in the next town over pulled a Chihuahua from a pool filter. That was the same storm that killed Sharon Franklin's grandfather. He was an old Navajo, time-worn with clouds in his eyes. He died of heart failure in a coat closet.

Civilization ground to a halt. The earth stuck out its tongue and revealed a mouthful of chaos. There was a cockeyed splendor to it all. The plains and the silence held ideas then, inside the motion of the ruins, rising and falling in that mute reverie that persists below the noise and bouncing thoughts. Silence. Outside of the weight of the voice that rambles in my head, there is a soothing quiet that cannot be defined, but even this quiet is not the silence that exists below the chatter and the movement of civilization. It is too often accompanied by a honking Honda Accord or the wind caught in the gutters. Even sitting deep in the wilderness I hear the occasional helicopter or bush plane. But immediately after a storm, when all the planes are grounded, the cars are parked, and the air conditioners are spread across three counties, you look out over the devastation and the silence consumes you.

Some people say that the Garden of Eden decayed below Oklahoma, and that's how the state came to be so oil rich, as if it were a gift from God given to the executives at Devon and Chesapeake Energy. I don't know who says that, but I've heard it somewhere. I couldn't tell you if Eden is flowing through the black oil below the clay and shale, but I know something about the weather in Oklahoma that comes down when the empty sky gets full and overflows. When the storms rise up over the great flatness that defines the western horizon and a deep gray swallows the sky, turning the sun's heat into a muck that fills the air between your fingers and toes. Over the fields of Oklahoma, the storms are all-consuming and merciless, emerging from a guttural blackness that spreads without warning and leaves towns in ruin. The lightning over the plains releases a cracked shrieking unique to the region, more robust and threatening, more kinetic than anything I've seen further west. The thunder makes your guts shift in your stomach, and the flash covers the surface of the earth for miles. In the moments following the strike, the remnants linger over everything in an afterglow that sizzles and pulses then fades away.

Then one day, under all this mean weather, the earth began to shake.

In my apartment, I swept away the mud I tracked in the day before—now a small pile of dirt—I swept it out the door where the rain fell from the roof, dripping in a frantic cadence, and I wondered if summer cared enough for my bitter solitude to reveal itself soon. The plains are hot and dry, but they have rains that come with a fierceness, rains that carry away your memories of drought on transient streams running along the streets and into storm drains, only to rise when heat and thirst consume you again. The off-colored thoughts that creep in during those long periods of summer sweat subside when the wild showers return. I left the door open and let the smell of rain cleanse my home. You could call it a home. I did for a time, but like many homes it became host to unwanted guests. Some came from outside my doors and some were of my own making.

Morning meant meditation on the eggs in the skillet, watering the basil in the kitchen, and staring at dust in the dawn with Erik Satie. These things made sense sometimes. What the day would bring did not, though I tried to piece it together with manic speculation. I was certain things could be better if I persevered, but that sort of wishful thinking leads to a miserable collection of days that you come to call a life, and I was way too afraid of my own mortality to allow for such a prolonged misstep.

The thunderstorms that electrify the plains are like white teeth chewing everything all at once, swallowing that university town, Norman, home of all God's errant children thrown to the wolves clutching their liberal arts degrees. You could look in every direction at a flatness that submits only to the curve of the planet, and all you see are dark, bubbling clouds.

Zach was asleep on the couch. He loved his dogs and grew peppers in his garden that trapped drought and the heat of the plains in their seeds. For several months of the year, the heat of those seeds overtook every meal he cooked. His thoughts ran away from him sometimes, and he disliked the way he spoke, the way his mind presented its contents to the world, but no one judged him for it more than himself.

As the moon rose, his eyes disappeared into his head and he jerked with nods, seeing through his eyelids, observing his surroundings, noting slight shifts in the mood until the entire night was swallowed inside the murk of his memory. Something inside made it impossible for him to disregard the empty souls floating in and out of his orbit, the well-meaning addicts that pushed their urges upward toward his line of vision so that he couldn't look away, and he himself verged on addiction, constantly walking a tightrope with a long fall waiting on either side. So when he needed a couch or a drinking buddy, I was there.

That morning his opioid fog was wearing off and things were clear and the TV fell from the dresser and he jumped from the couch—the windows chattering like epileptics. Then it was gone, and I watched him fall back to sleep, but the earthquakes were not going to stop. After the deep-injection wells were built, the number of earthquakes increased at a startling rate—almost 900%. Four of the five worst earthquakes in the state's recorded history were triggered by over three-billion gallons of that salty, benzene-laced shit. It still spreads through old faults and crevices, diffusing deep into the Arbuckle formation and then deeper still into the so-called *basement*.

Oklahoma is no stranger to shaking ground. In 1995, Timothy McVeigh blew a hole in the side of the Alfred P. Murrah Federal Building, killing 168 people, including 19 children. My dad still talks about that day. He was working in the courthouse downtown when the ground shuddered, and the building was evacuated. While filing through the emergency exits with the other evacuees, he noticed that something was different about the federal building. He couldn't place it, but he kept staring. Then it struck him. He walked out of that courthouse day-after-day and in all that time he never saw light shining through the windows of the Murrah building. Then he understood what had happened, that the other side of the building was gone. The morning sun was caught up in gray clouds, giving a dull glow to the drywall, floor tiles, and insulation raining on the streets of downtown Oklahoma City. What I'm trying to say is, for Oklahomans, shaking ground is a symptom of attack.

I drove to Mount Ida to dig for quartz one summer when my feet were itching due to the monotony of the day job. The way the landscape changes as you head east into the Ozark Mountains is sudden and dramatic. The plains break and there is moisture to the vegetation that can't be found on the prairies to the west. At a pit stop, a young woman sold jewelry made from Arkansas quartz wrapped in copper wire, paired with turquoise, amethyst, or agate. She told me there was a mega vortex underneath Mount Ida, and this small Ozark town was the portal of the quantum crystalline frequency where the wisdom of the great Atlantean crystal was pushing upward toward the earth's surface, and that's where all the quartz was coming from, remnants of the great crystal that powered the lost city of Atlantis arriving through interdimensional tunnels. She told me that there were blue-skinned beings still traveling underneath Arkansas, living freely among the tunnels. She called them LeMurians.

The quartz appeared as a flash piercing the red clay, sending a beam of bent, refracted light up from the ground like glass eyes of variegated sizes, shaped by darkness and peering fully into the Arkansas sun for the first time as I dusted them off with an old horse-hair paint brush. It was an active, bursting light, unable to contain its reaction to the first glimpses of the atmosphere. The woman at the convenience store told me quartz shined in the sun only if it wanted to be found. The trees above grew sparingly from the clay and the canopy was thinly leafed, so the sun had no trouble making its way to the back of my neck, and I could feel it turning pink. I wrapped it in a wet bandana. It was red and stained with blood from a stick that went through my foot on a fishing trip along the Canadian River. I carried a piece of that stick inside me for years until it fell out while I was dancing at a rave in Kansas City.

The tools I used for mining quartz were simple. I held the horse-hair paint brush and a rusted screwdriver with a worn wooden handle. I kicked anything shiny and dusted it off. If it was something worth digging up, I stabbed the screwdriver into the red earth and pried it from the ground. I walked away with a small bag full of cloudy quartz.

That night, I slept next to the Ouachita River under towering elms in a worn out Marmot tent, and the rain came down so hard that the whole structure nearly collapsed on top of me as I curled up next to my sack of Atlantean crystals having visions of lost cities and blue-skinned people. I camped on a piece of private property with a large sign that read *Two Spirit Campground*, and the guy who owned the place was quick to point out that it was named for the loving relationship he had with his wife, and it was only later he found out that Two Spirit also meant "something like a gay Indian."

The river flooded and I woke up next to the water.

It is hard to believe all the moments that slip away from me. Moments that I lose to time and never reclaim, but the world sat down beside me that morning. I was breathing easy on a log being devoured by soil, still wet from the rain that had come overnight and chilled, covering the tent in a layer of frost that left as morning broke upon the river and all of it glimmered. I was idle while dawn faded, and everything dissolved exactly as it should. There were moments when the clouds became layered and they could not rest, picking up speed and allowing themselves the liberty of a quick getaway to the east where they would split and percolate in oozing patterns among the wooded Ozark peaks. When everything is gone, leveled as they say, it is only the plains and its holes that exist, a panorama of the great colonial letdown that pushes things to the surface—the crystals and oil and anxieties that run between all things but don't wish to be seen.

The sound of a tornado from the fetal position on the bathroom floor is like a freight train big enough to carry God. The light is like staring at the sun through a brown cotton blanket, but the feeling that rises up inside when the tornado is on top of you, I don't have words for that. No metaphor. No simile. Nothing to compare. It is pure emotion, pure sense beyond language.

There are ways of observing the world and predicting patterns of weather, though they are becoming less reliable in the age of ecocide. Before Doppler radar and satellites and smartphones, Grandma Owens paid attention to the wildlife and the subtle movements of ecology. If there was a red sky at sunset, or the flowers were pushing out a sweet smell, if the frogs were croaking louder and the ants were building higher while the spiders dropped lower, Grandma knew that rain was on its way. But if the birds were flying high and the grass was covered in morning dew under white clouds, she assured us that the weather would be clear for a while. In these ways, the world speaks to us.

The world is changing and with it the patterns of ecology are changing too. I might have a hard time convincing Uncle Jim that climate change and all the catastrophe that comes with it are bearing down on us, but I don't have to tell the pika. They already know. They are fleeing to higher elevations every single year. I don't have to pull up the latest IPCC report for the European bee-eaters who are pushing through longer and longer migrations. And the grizzly bears who are on an endless, futile quest for disappearing pine nuts don't need to be convinced by tropospheric carbon dioxide readings. They know what's happening, and they can show us.

Still, there are things that wildlife can't tell us. They can't point out all the minutiae of ecocide. There should have never been major earthquakes in a tornado state. Not in my lifetime. I've heard this geological era called many things: the Anthropocene, the Capitalocene, the Necrocene, the Chthulucene. It is all of these things, the age of humans, of capital, of death, of weird all-encompassing diabolical monsters.

Despite this, many Oklahomans are uniquely capable of overlooking these warning signs. There are folks still alive who witnessed the carnage of the Dust Bowl, the children coughing and choking to death, the homes buried in dry and barren topsoil but they ignore the earth shaking beneath their feet. I met a Kansan in a bar in Missoula who was puffy-eyed and doughy-cheeked, and he had a real jubilant way of moving his arms in tune with his words that made me want to talk to him for hours. He said, "I wish you Okies would stop giving us your God damned earthquakes." We are regularly reminded of the destruction that the planet can bring down upon people, whether that be the dust storms that plagued the state nearly a century ago or the tornadoes that steal away homes and photo albums and family bibles.

Grandma Owens has a new home on a half-acre. She sits on her back porch every evening watching birds and talking to the homeless tortoiseshell cat that hides in the hickory next to her shed. That cat drives her dog, Darcy, wild. Darcy ends up choking on her own barking fit and steaming up the glass panes with her nose pressed against the backdoor. If she gets out, which she sometimes does, she blazes a path cleared by bloodlust toward that cat, and the thing just waits there in a way that's intentionally aggravating until Darcy is no more than a few feet away. Then the tortoiseshell climbs the wood pallet that's always leaned against the shed and hops on the roof while Darcy continues to lose her damn mind there on the ground.

An hour or so after the tornado hit the wind picked up again, and I stood looking over the alien ruins with chapped lips cracking like lightning. Over the Cross Timbers into the sea of broken homes and lives ripped from the ground, I saw the destructive power of wild things. And in the face of that wildness, civilization and empire seemed delicate. A tear opened in that bent silence, and a wind behind it let out an ancient shriek that hit my senses and sailed across a ravine chiseled along a timeline stretching so far that I could not imagine it. I felt the silence, and it was the sound of a world without us. That silence was at once awe-inspiring and horrible. There is no shade on the plains, only the sun and the relentless wind that never fails to make itself known. I've felt many winds, but those on the plains rush over my skin in a way that is unique and uninterrupted, bringing water to my eyes. It's at its worst in February, walking down Asp Avenue through the University of Oklahoma where the mathematics building and the fine arts library form a howling tunnel. When everything is said and done and the dark skies are gone, I send my mind with them toward night and emptiness. I try to think about more delicious things than what I've seen, but every time my eyes return to the Oklahoma

City skyline it brings about its own tornado inside me that leaves the cocaine spilt on the passenger seat, and a friend by my side howling to the golden idol of progress. Everything I love is disappearing—we all cope in our own ways.

THE WITCH OF KITCHEN LAKE

———————

The crackling sound of burning wood, the heat on his face, the smell of beef and battery acid cooking in a frying pan. Then a wave of heat and the sulfuric stench of burnt hair. That's all there was. The Settler's eyes were squeezed close.

He opened them to a sky that was supple and orange. Everyone's voices clamoring. The world was liberated of another impurity. The accused isolated herself in the shadows of the Cross Timbers, but her isolation was not enough. There was no forgiveness for those who communed with the devil and lusted for earthly things, the pleasures of the body, invoking an occult connection to the natural world. That made her an enemy of the divine. There'd be no trial. It wasn't Salem. It was outlaw country. Society's laws had no hold.

A group of men took it upon themselves to do the Lord's bidding. They crossed over the old bridge near Kitchen Lake, fifteen maybe twenty of them. The Settler didn't think to count. It was simple: they couldn't have a witch out there in those woods where their kids ran around. They couldn't trust a woman who lived alone in the darkness of the woods anyhow. Witch or not, there was something not right about a woman behaving that way.

The Settler had heard stories. The people in those parts, they talk-ed a lot, tales whispered through the years—cries of children coming from her home, mad fires with mysterious figures dancing naked in the flames, demonic specters mingling with the tangled shadows of the hickories, non-human things standing upright and moving around like a man would, beastly grumbling in response to vile promises, wailing pleasure, copulating with wild animals.

She grew a wicked garden of hallucinogenic plants and herbs that could heal the flesh through the Devil's blessing. They passed it as they approached the little old cottage. Tufts of smoke rose from the stone chimney.

They slammed their fists against the door. She cracked it open and peered out. A few of the men forced their way in and pinned her down. She was screaming, kicking, biting, grabbing. She kept asking what the reason was for all this. She kept denying her ungodliness. They tied her up. The Settler started to feel a little off after a while. All that screaming and crying made something like guilt creep up. They got in that mob with everybody going along with all the hoop-la, and he felt compelled to keep it going. That's what the Settler did, just stood complacent in the whole thing. Still, he felt he was in need of some penance.

He'd never forget the burning. It haunted him. The moment the fire started to pop and the smell of red oak hit his nose, the Settler knew there was no going back. His thoughts raced like a greyhound, pulling far ahead so he couldn't keep up. He tried to take deep breaths. The finality set in. The Settler squeezed his eyes closed until the whole thing was over.

This brief saga of depravity is said to have unfolded past the bridge at Kitchen Lake, a few miles south of Tinker Air Force Base. It is a tale that has been caught up and chewed by the jaws of time and the minds of teenagers. The story of a fire and a haunting.

A silver cross swung from my neck as I squeezed my knees together beside Loren with his dry, Percocet eyes and his thin frame, shifting skin and bone in baggy black shorts. This was before a stomach pump and a brief stint in rehab left him thinking the Marines could give his life some purpose. His tour in Afghanistan broke him. He didn't have the disposition to cope with that kind of violence. It takes a dark force to tear up a person's mind like that. He was discharged, and he returned home to find his dad dying of pancreatic cancer. Nothing could be done about it. Some people just get a bad hand.

His Nissan truck rumbled and creaked on its worn suspension. A cowboy killer hung from his thin lips, bouncing loosely between long drags that made his cheeks cave so his face appeared hollow and skeletal. Spots of acne added to his gritty appeal.

Loren's girlfriend Anna sat on the other side of me in a tight red shirt that was frayed above her belly button, which was adorned with a butterfly jewel. She was always keen and bubbly. After high school, she moved to LA so she didn't have to hide her intellect anymore.

The washboard road kicked my diaphragm around in my chest. Odd, fractal vapor gyrated, swirling around the wings of a dancing scissor-tail flycatcher, then drifted further along the red and green shores of Kitchen Lake. Scattered piles of ash marked the dirt road that ran two miles to the decaying bridge, burn piles where ranchers and sadistic teenagers had set fire to animals, living and dead. Others were the charred remains of beer bottles, children's toys, diapers, and phonebooks. The warm air smelled like a roll of pennies. The result of blood vessels and spinal fluid. It was a place of fire.

The sunset painted the surface of the water with an orange that noted the shadows among the swells in ways that were distinct but approached the shoreline with an ease and a softness. I watched a fish touch the surface. It made the water look like bent glass that moved toward the shore. A willow caught the ripples on the surface, split them, and shook slightly in the wind.

The perimeter fence had been snipped by renegade anglers unwilling to pay a fee to fish the waters of the private lake. We would take a six pack and our rods, sliding them through the cut barbed wire. We got skunked nine times out of ten, but every once in a while, we reeled in a small mouth bass or a fat crappie. Sitting on the shore one morning, I watched a school of sand bass flopping on the surface. The water appeared to boil, like rain was falling from the lake bottom up toward the sky. We would walk the north shore scouting for patrols that hassled us for trespassing. We'd spot them on their ATVs before they made it to the dense woods on the western side and flee through the bluestem grass, trying to keep our tackle boxes held together and gulping down our beers before we got to the car.

We arrived at the end of the road where the burn piles became too numerous to maneuver the truck through. It was another quarter mile to the bridge. We stepped into the muggy night and weaved through charred piles of bone and flesh and hair, metal barrels filled with ash and singed newspapers. One with an old article, half burned, about the trials of Terry Nichols and Timothy McVeigh. We came to Kitchen Lake Bridge which had withered away, leaving only two thick beams still set in place. We balanced with our arms extended, carefully placing one foot in front of the other as we walked over them. Below us were the remnants of a waterway asphyxiated by Kitchen Lake Dam. Moist earth is all that's left of that creek—a red mud that will stain your feet for days.

The only lights for miles shined from Tinker Air Force Base. A radiating metropolis of military force, it generated a dense glow, penetrating the sky and pressing into the pale blue shining from the half moon. Military aircraft would come and go at all hours, armed to the teeth with explosives and surveillance technology. A fence stretched for miles and miles around the entire complex, all entrances heavily guarded by camouflaged soldiers carrying automatic weapons. A sinister acropolis.

As we crossed the bridge, I shined my heavy Maglite north into a tunnel of green and black lined with breathing shadows that grew endlessly darker until they swallowed the glow of the flashlight. Loren slipped and caught himself, but his light tumbled into the creek bed. He hung down, stretched between the steel beams, then let go and fell into the undergrowth ten feet below. We heard him wrestle through the brush, cursing and stumbling until he located his flashlight and shined it into the sky yelling, "I'm good! I'm good! I'll meet you on the other side."

We crossed the bridge and found Loren back on solid ground before pushing through a thick stand of chokeberry that was glowing and alive. Aside from several small pockets of gravel along the way, there was little sign of the old road that once weaved through trees and shrubs and grass. The canopy inched toward reconnection over the past half-century, and it looked like the limbs finally came to intermingle within the last decade or so. There were bones of cattle and squirrels and dogs strung up in the trees. The moon cast a glow that wrestled with the darkness of the forest on either side of us.

We pushed forward until the trees suddenly opened and we saw the remains of an old cottage. A chimney rose from a broken fireplace on a deteriorated floor. The last erect totem among the ruins of the isolated home. They say the witch was burned at this place for communing with the devil. The scene played out again and again in my mind. The witch dancing naked among the tangled shadows of oaks, the flickering flames causing the webbed specters to pulsate madly, but all of that is conjecture. It's a story that has been told to coat the tragic with the fantastical.

There was no witch. Truth is, the entire area was burned to the ground in the late 1940s due to jet fuel spilled by the Air Force base. The octane levels left an odd stench that lingered in the air for years. Over the next decade, the American military became responsible for over a quarter of the world's energy consumption. It unleashed Fat Man and Little Boy, ushering in the era of nuclear armament. Entire cities, ecosystems could disappear with the flick of a hand.

Stories of Sasquatches and ghosts and lake monsters with writhing tentacles circle the dinner tables and barstools of the plains, while the earth shakes below our feet, echoing the residual effects of deep-injection wells. It is no surprise that the legend of Kitchen Lake is pure fantasy and that the truth of the matter is indicative of a problem more sinister and far-reaching than witchcraft, enshrouded in more black magic than Marie Laveau or Morgan Le Fay or the Witch of Kitchen Lake.

Witches in the time of enlightenment were burned for the crime of infanticide. Our understanding of the casualties of war, of collateral damage, has changed over the last century with the advent of more destructive technology that coincided with our embrace of hyper-militarism. Thirty-two percent of Iraqi civilians killed in coalition airstrikes between 2003 and 2006 were under the age of fifteen. I guess the puritans were right. Some black magic does require child sacrifice before it comes bubbling from the ground.

I looked through the gallery of graffiti painted onto the floor and the trees. All the old clichés were accounted for: 666, hail Satan, so-and-so loves so-and-so, swastikas, racial epithets. There was one wholesome rebel who stuck with Jesus Saves, but someone had marked out saves and replaced it with sucks, and below that someone else scribbled dicks. Just to clarify. There was a gas can on the ground. I picked it up. Shook it. Empty.

I stared into the sky where the lights of the Air Force base killed the stars. Toward the vast, esoteric strings connecting the leviathan of military, connections of forbidden insight that control past, present, and future across the planet. They exist outside of spatial and temporal confines. The divination of certain outcomes comes at a cost, a blood sacrifice and a whetting and baiting of fear and patriotic discontent. While war has become messier and more impersonal, more a matter of business and profit than heroism and defense, the over-funded branch of US empire has become the number one source of pollution in the world.

Those AWACs that soar daily through Oklahoma's sky burn 2,625 gallons of jet fuel an hour. That's about forty-four gallons a minute. As a child, I lay in the grass counting them as they took off one after another to carry out whatever covert mission they were tasked with that day. And it wasn't only AWACs, it was B-1s, B-2s, A-10s, AC-130s, and B-52s, hell-hurdling beasts and fuming harpies invoked by gruff generals with sagging cheeks and a conscience that's always clear.

It's not just the process of war that is characterized by environmental degradation but the very aim of it. Most of our militaristic ventures into other countries can be charted by looking at their wealth of natural resources. Of course, many Americans don't believe that. They accept the idea that we are spreading freedom by fighting terror and authoritarianism, persecuting a savage religion in Islam or a dangerous ideology in socialism. It's been over four hundred years since the Salem witch trials, and the evangelicals that haunt this country remain prone to the same puritanical mass hysteria.

Witches and pagans had little use for hierarchy, especially as solitary practitioners. They communicated with animals, plants, dirt, and stone, all of which they understood as being imbued with spirit. This animistic view of empowerment undermined the rigid power structures of monotheistic religions and the patriarchal institutions that grew from them. It gave autonomy to the woman as an individual. She communed with the spirits of the earth. This empowerment explains why folk magic has been wielded historically as a form of resistance against subjugation, against empire and slavery. Hierarchies on a scale both grand and small are the model for the American military, whether that be American exceptionalism or a colonel who punishes a private. To lead by fear rather than cooperation and mutual aid.

After we finished sifting through animal bones and inspecting graffiti, we sat in a row with our legs hanging from the edge of the crumbling floor.

"You ever wonder why, of all places, we were born here?" Anna asked.

"Bad luck," Loren said.

"Yeah, but do you think we were supposed to learn something? Like maybe we kinda fucked up in our last life," Anna asked.

"Maybe we burned a witch," I said.

"I guess what I'm saying is that we were born around all these people who don't seem to give a shit about anything but themselves. All those people in the state capitol like that prick Scott Pruitt. Is this a test to see if we'll cave in and turn into assholes too?" Anna asked.

"Yeah, maybe we gave in and became assholes in our last life, so that's why we were born in Oklahoma," I said.

"That means this is an important conversation, right? It marks the moment we became aware of the Great Cycle of Assholes, so we're pretty close to transcending it. Maybe in my next life I can be born in Hawaii or on a Greek Island," Anna said.

"It doesn't matter where you're born in the next life. It's all going to be ash by the time we make it through the bardo. We're too late. We were assholes for one too many lives," Loren said.

The chirping crickets were joined by a bullfrog giving voice to the mute blackness spilling from the woods. The lightning bugs lit up in the forest like dust from another dimension. The military has its own dust simmering in the sands of Iraq. Nearly four million pounds of depleted uranium coalesce with the country's dunes, poisoning Iraqi citizens and American soldiers alike. With a half-life of four and a half billion years, the sands of Iraq will sing a radioactive song long after the human race has perished, and as it finally loses its charge, our galaxy will be experiencing the death of the Sun.

Several millennia before they were diluted by depleted uranium, those sands served as the cradle of civilization. The Sumerians of what is now Southern-Iraq were responsible for the earliest Neolithic settlements. The very first sign of the political society, which overtook the kinship systems that were typical of pre-Neolithic societies and eventually became the primitive prototype for what is today's global capitalist system. Systems of slavery were set up, so there was a surplus of goods beyond that which was needed for consumption. Hence, the idea of profit and eventually the pursuit of wealth through global warfare once military technology caught up to our drive for the accumulation of resources.

Stateside, the US military has a long, kooky, relationship with the desert that has given rise to new myths and cosmologies like ours at Kitchen Lake. The presence of civilization in the desert could not counteract its inherent weirdness. It only fed into the myth of the UFO, one which the military could promote to draw the public's attention away from their own top-secret experiments, leading to reports of black triangles, floating orbs, and flying saucers. The military is the great architect behind this American mythology. They have their hands on the shaping of the collective American psyche, deciding what is seen and what is rendered invisible.

I've had my own experiences with peculiar things seen in the night sky. Sitting in the grass outside of my grandparents' house I watched a long green fiery streak creep from the upper atmosphere and disappear before it hit the horizon. I wrote it off as the burning pieces of a satellite or some other space debris, though it moved more like honey on a windowpane than a flashing meteor. Some years later, I came across the research of Dr. Lincoln LaPaz. These so-called green fireballs have been a cause of concern for the US Air Force since the 1950s, as they often appear in close proximity to US military installations. My Grandma Owens's house was less than a mile from Tinker Air Force Base. The government believed that these green fireballs were linked to Soviet espionage campaigns. Project Twinkle was established to study the fireballs and they were deemed natural in origin though the cause was never identified. Until his death, Dr. LaPaz maintained that the phenomenon was artificial. He looked at his critics stern-jawed over his dark mustache and maintained that he, as a man who had spent a lifetime studying the qualities of meteors, was certain that this was no natural phenomenon. They moved differently. They lit up the sky in unnatural ways.

I looked up to the sky then. A glow. The forest. A blackness. Loren. The hollow. Anna. The wonder. Our feet hung from the side of the crumbling structure, swinging above green grass growing from ash and dirt. You dig in and you'll find that the clay is red and rich with iron like blood. I hopped and landed upon that Oklahoma earth, for a century plagued by its own clandestine abundance. We began walking back to the truck.

In a bleak irony, the American military has openly embraced the reality of climate change. The reason for this is two-fold. One, they know, unequivocally, that it is happening. Two, they know that they can use it as an excuse for increased militarism in the future. There will be wars over resources and there will be climate refugees. Valuable new territories will emerge, so-called *cold deserts* exposed by the melting of the arctic. Industrial interests wouldn't pass on this chance to fully embrace a new reason for warfare, conquest, and, above all, profit. Resource depletion and militarism are inseparable. They sustain one another.

Our minds began to play tricks on us as we moved back toward the bridge, and I looked up to see flames rising from the truck. Loren and Anna saw them too. It appeared first like a raging inferno in the distance. We ran over piles of burned magazines and soda bottles, through half-charred animal remains, knocking over steel drums, blackened and lacerated. But as we got closer, the flames got smaller, like a lantern hovering above the ground. In the corner of my eye, there were flashes of dog skulls hanging from the tree limbs as darkness oozed through the vegetation. Viscous black coursing through the veins of night. The flame grew smaller still, a glowing pinprick, like the keyhole into a furnace room, culminating in an endless pursuit.

The story of sustainability begins with a myth. It's found-ed upon a fable, brutal and barbaric, that we can liberate ourselves from the worst parts of civilization through the mechanisms of capital and electoralism. Mythologies are propped up so we don't have to cope with the truth that our planet is suffering. We are told that if we recycle, transition to solar, write letters to our senators, things will be ok. What we see now is the most radical expression of the instability of western civilization. The more we pursue the promises of sustainability, the further out of reach our chance for survival becomes. Even if every single person on the globe stopped consuming and emitting, the world's military forces, war itself, consumes and emits enough pollutants to push us forward into the spiral of catastrophic climate change with feedback loops, mass extinction, and fire—unstoppable fire.

When we made it back to the truck, we were dazed and wondering what exactly happened. It must have been a reflection on the rims or the side view mirror that dimmed as we got closer. It must have been the excitement, the way sound or light can be exacerbated by the tension of the moment. We slid into the cab and looked at each other. What had we just seen? Some illusion. A shared hallucination, certainly.

When Loren got back from his tour in Afghanistan, we met at Booger Red's for a drink. I thanked him for his tour of duty. He looked into his beer, fidgeting uncomfortably under the weight of my empty expression of gratitude.

"Come on man. I know you too well to believe that you're 'thankful for my service.' You think the war is bullshit, and you know what? You're right. It is bullshit. But all that violence... It sticks with me..."

He swallowed some of his Coors.

"You know what's weird, though? Nothing really changed here in the time between when I left and when I got back. This country doesn't even know we're at war. Not really. It's not like World War II or Vietnam, when you came back and they loved you or hated you."

He adjusted the wet napkin underneath his glass.

"We've been at war for so long, and with nobody really. Y'all don't even remember it's happening. Why would you? That's what they want, isn't it? What was that Chomsky shit you used to rattle on about, manufacturing consent? But...it's just that, us, the ones that went over there, we still see what's invisible to most of you. We still know. We still know that the war is happening and it's just as fucked up as it always was."

Many of the tragedies of war now go unreported. They are unseen, unnoticed. Lives are lost and minds are left in need of mending. The environmental toll will eventually lead to a new reality where fires burn year around and, as Americans, we see nothing. All that jet-fuel consumed Kitchen Lake in a vast inferno, and the military is still setting fire to the world.

Kitchen Lake is red. Saturated in Oklahoma's dirt. When the water's surface is calm, you can see the flying machinery of war reflected back into the sky. Nothing goes unacknowledged. The grass and the limbs of the willows grow long around its shores, bending with shifting winds toward the borders of this country, toward an invisible war in every direction. The planes take off and they land. Inside the Air Force base there are homes and grocery stores and bowling alleys. There is a golf course and a liquor store. The sandwich shops proudly offer military discounts, making change for a turkey club under the watchful eye of the American flag. There is a vision for a future based on a past that never was. What a country.

Every morning Loren wakes up and makes a cup of tea. He sweeps. The silence is nice. He distrusts his senses. Walking through his garden, he talks to his plants. He sits with them, and he tells them good morning.

YOUNG MEN AND FISH

There is a trout camp in Gore where my family went on summer vacation when I was young and trying to understand the things that made the world good. We swam and fished and crossed the Arkansas River on quarter horses when the water was low. Old fishermen slept in beat up campers near the riverbank, drinking Bud under the shade of their awnings and wading into the water to catch rainbows before the dam opened in late afternoon. It was on the banks of the Arkansas flowing through Gore where I learned walleye have teeth. People appreciate trout like they appreciate walleye. The president of Trout Unlimited makes over a quarter million dollars a year. I hope he is saving a few fish with that salary, because I'm certain he is catching them. Trash fish aren't so lucky. Carp, drum, gar, suckers, and chubs—no one makes a six-figure salary to protect them.

The river was low. The dam was closed. A grizzled man with a feather earring slouched in a camper chair outside his RV. His hair hadn't been cut in a decade or more, aside from what time had taken from him. He said the alligator gar were spawning in a tributary to the southeast.

"Took a jaunt to where they're all pooled up. Not a bad walk. Bit of bushwhacking. But they won't bite nothing, man. Not even live bait. They have their minds on other things, know what I'm saying? If you think you're gonna catch something on a lure, forget it. Not a chance."

Gar are the creatures of nightmares, beautiful things, long and brutish fish with sharp teeth hanging from their mouths in a jagged expanse that filled me with fear when I was young and swimming in the waters of Oklahoma. Gar have fins the size of a Neanderthal's head after it was flattened by a well-rounded stone some 40,000 years ago when they were swimming these same waters. Their bodies stretch long like the plains, and they are thick and strong.

Gar break the surface to breathe the hot Oklahoma air. It's a unique trait. They have fully functioning gills, yet they prefer a variety of breathing patterns, as yogic masters do. Their bladders function as lungs. Occasionally, when they surface, there will be a hillbilly with a bow and arrow waiting for them. The arrow is connected to a long line used to reel them in once it's sunk. After you get one with a bow, it has little chance of surviving, but they put up a notoriously good fight, bleeding and twisting, struggling until their last moment when life escapes them and they are left to the whims of the current. I don't know why the bow fishermen waste them. Gar are said to be good eating.

I used to tease my sister when she was in the water behind the boat on Tenkiller Lake, skiing or inner tubing. "You know there are gar in there. They're probably swimming below your feet right now."

"No, they aren't. Are they?!" she screamed.

I laughed and Dad told me to shut up.

Gar get a bad rap perhaps because they have a sinister look about them.

Thick riparian vegetation crowded the shoreline. I pushed my way through the undergrowth carrying a rod over my head. It kept getting caught on the sassafras and spicebush. I came across a baby vulture. Its feathers were a light brown, and its head stuck from its body like a pruned toe in the bathtub. It seemed startled. Some biological inclination struck panic into its being, feeling a certainty deep down that if it stayed there too long a coyote was going to have its way with it. I looked up to see if there was a nest in the canopy. Nothing.

Pressing forward, the water was warm and slow enough to wade across to the eastern shore. The stones pressed into the arches of my bare feet. I followed a fork in the river, continuing east for half a mile across smooth rock. Thin grass was growing tall between the stones, but there were no trees. I watched a crawdad poking out from its hole, shoveling detritus into its mouth and playing an invisible piano with eight skinny legs upon the river rock.

Then I came to the pool filled with gar. The tributary was shallow and clear, and the gar were big. Magnified by the clarity of the water, their four feet looked like six feet, their six feet like eight feet, writhing and flopping. I dropped a worm right in the middle hoping to get a bite, but they were transfixed by their sexual impulses. They'd waited a long time for this. All those bow hunters stuck them in the side and pulled them to shore, so I figured I could do something like that. If I used a big hook, I could sink it between the ribs and reel it in. I'd find out if what they say about gar meat is true. I tasted carp at a Czech Christmas party after it spent the week prior shitting in Jana's bathtub, and if I could stomach that, I could swallow just about anything.

Gar have navigated these waters for millennia. They are slow to pass themselves on, as the females can't reproduce until they are a decade old, but this long period of infertility has served their longevity. Alongside sturgeon, they are one of the oldest species of fish existing today, dating back to the Paleocene. Humanity's accelerated evolutionary rate is indicative of an early extinction. Our rapid growth, our never-ending interspecies colonization indicates that we aren't adapted for longevity. Gar, on the other hand, take their time, bathing in the uncertainty of existence rather than consuming and eradicating it. Gar have been mythologized. People say they grow twenty feet long and feed on unsuspecting swimmers. They are the great sea serpent of southern folklore.

After casting a few times with no success, I gave up and waded into the water. The gar moved around me in wild, roiling patterns. I felt their age in the interlocking circles they swam around my legs. I felt life cycles creeping through millennia, tied to their ancient memories of copulation, birth, and death. Where the flowing water of the river stopped, still and glasslike, I felt one hundred million years of genetic history flopping and splashing water into the air, chomping at the bit with bestial energy. Thousands of razor-sharp teeth could have left me lying in strips. They rubbed against my legs, against my feet, and they ignored me just like any other bait. The eternal flow of the river stopped in that place, and I was in contact with the endlessness. For a moment, everything was clear standing among those trash fish.

Follow the Arkansas River past Gore toward the Mississippi and you'll come to the Ozark Dam where they opened the spillways and killed 100,000 freshwater drum fish. They died from gas bubble trauma. 100,000 dead fish washed up on the banks of the Arkansas. Drum are called trash fish too. They have an otolith in their head, a unique ear bone that many people call a lucky stone.

I used to fish with Sid day and night. He was a wild man who swung and moved among the limbs of trees like a feral acrobat. After high school, Sid enlisted in the military and shattered a leg during a parachute landing in Tarinkot, but as soon as it healed he was back in the sandbox, as they say. I never understood it. I always figured him for a resolute anarchist.

We were on the water with Sid's family late one night. The boat was tied to a wide bridge passing high above Lake Texoma. The sound of the vehicles overhead triggered a hollow, chugging vibration that bounced between our ears as we sloshed around under a dark sky, rubbing against black water, all of it illuminated by the reflection of the streetlamps and a full moon. We reeled in plenty of bass and catfish, which was cause for celebration, but the drum fish were subjected to someone's idea of a game. A barbaric test of might. The challenge was to knock the lucky stone loose from the center of the fish's head. This was done by hurling it against the side of the boat or the concrete pillar that anchored us. It was easy to identify the males because they made a grunting noise when they were pulled from the water—the sound of their muscles beating against their gas bladder. The fish panicked, sliding between Sid's hands, groaning and spreading their gills as he grabbed the tail fin and went to work. If the lucky stone was jostled free from the thin layer of flesh between the fish's eyes, it made a bloop noise as it splashed into the water, and on calm nights, you could see the ripples in the moon's reflection. The fish were left to bleed out in the up and down of the water's surface, still warm from the summer sun. Perhaps more concerning to me now, looking back, is not those that lost their otolith, but the fish that were beaten only to swim away with broken bones and brain damage.

I never asked how they came across this biological trait, or its ability to so readily take leave of a drum fish's forehead. I said nothing. Just sat and smirked, mildly entertained by the spectacle of savagery, watching them bounce off the boat, twisting and contorting as they ricocheted through the air.

Of course, my turn came. I caught a drum and pulled it from deep in the water until its scales shined in the spotlight below the surface. I jerked up on the rod and it emerged and I saw its gills expand and I heard its gas bladder being beat by its insides. It flopped midair at the end of the line. I pulled it into the boat. I knew what was expected of me. I gripped the drum by the tail. Its scales felt smooth then rough inside my hands as it curled. Its lidless eyes did not move. It sucked in and it's gas bladder kept making that same noise, over and over. I was in the spotlight then. A wet thud against the fiberglass. No splash or ripples under the full moon. The drum fell into the water, probably braindead and still holding its lucky stone. I had lost. The drum had lost. We floated together, adrift. It's hard to say who's to blame for any of this. There seems to be some bloodlust carried in our genes before we're thrown into a world in which it's reinforced. It takes nothing short of an act of God, some trauma or mutation, to change that.

In the African-American hoodoo rituals of the South, lucky stones are used to conjure up good fortune. Maybe someone came across those lucky stones after they tumbled out of Lake Texoma and down the Red River, washing up on a Louisiana shore. Maybe they stuffed them deep into their mojo hand, and maybe they carry them still. Maybe the loa, Kalfu, who guards the crossroads, waves his bottle of rum and gunpowder at bad luck saying, "You can't cross here. Not if you're gonna be bothering this one." One can imagine such things. One can hope that some good comes from all of this.

We floated into the dock sometime around two AM. The boat was yellowed by time, worn down by sunlight, and it wasn't uncommon for the engine to putter out far from any boat ramp, leaving us to catch a tow back or use the troll motor to finally float to shore. The chill of night rode the southern wind across the turbid water, whistling through trees and between states. The swells pressed themselves into the reflection of the full moon, brighter now that night had aged a bit. Along the shore, tall grasses lurched and bent, flicking the water's surface. The night held a collective sway. No sooner did the wind move forward than did it turn around.

As the name indicates, Texoma straddles the state line. There is no small amount of animosity between the two states, so Okies like to brag that most of the lake rests north of the border. There was a funny feeling floating out there on the water in the dark and the quiet when things become borderless, and I felt a fine sense of displacement, a placelessness that I identified with.

Sid's dad was stout and bald, built on an athletic frame, and a deeply Christian man. Thirty pounds of fish hung from his right shoulder. We pulled in enough to feed the entire family at the fish fry the next day. There was a station at the marina where we cleaned them on small wooden cutting boards. It floated on rusted old pontoons, and the dock bumpers attached to them were cracked from dry rot.

We applied pressure to the fish bellies until they popped and the thin blade of the filet knife penetrated the scales. Blood oozed out and covered our hands as we pulled on the entrails, tossing them into the cove by the handful. We couldn't see the blood in the black water even with the moon so full. I pulled out a channel catfish that's belly was swollen with eggs. Her head was big and wide. Grandad Owens taught me to clean catfish on a rainy afternoon after the clouds came in fast while we were still on the lake. He held it against a tree and drove a six-inch nail through its head then cut out the filets with a Swiss army knife.

Some of the fish writhed until the very end. I don't know if it was life or nerves that made them do it. I was working out a nice little filet when I saw an ominous sort of rippling on the lake's surface. I looked closer. Had it been daytime, I could've seen what was crashing through the small waves coming and going with the breeze, but without the light, their twisting bodies, hungry and streaming with cytotoxic venom, blended into the blackness of the cove beside the blood and the guts. A den of water moccasins, a southern breed of pit viper, got worked up by all the entrails dumped into the waters of the marina. A fish cleaning station was a good spot for a water moccasin to den down. The waters were shallow and turbid, and they could live off the discarded scraps of the fishermen's catch.

It wasn't my first run-in with moccasins, but this bunch was aggressive, and there were dozens of them. They slithered onto the dock with quick, frantic curves tremoring through their bodies, propelling them forward, writhing and turning, tangling over one another in a blood-fueled delirium. The moments were moving fast, and I was having a hard time processing the gravity of the situation, but my arms and legs reacted with little help from my mind, throwing our things together, the filet knives, the boat key, my shoes. We pulled our bag of fish from the water and ran for the shore. A three-foot snake had its fangs dug into one of our sand bass. Sid's dad wielded his cutting board, crow-hopped, and swung for the fences. The snake sailed in rapid circles like the hands of a clock moving in fast forward, its body a blur in front of the moon. Moccasins were blocking our only hope of getting off the pier—a thin walkway with collapsing handrails. We joined him in swinging our wooden cutting boards, dripping red with blood. Every impact sent a snake hurdling into the water. We fought our way to shore. We kept running through the parking lot until we were clear on the other side. We dropped the paddles into the grass, now stained with the blood of both snake and fish. We stood tall with our hands interlocked behind our heads, winded and still tingling.

I wonder, what is the meanness of young boys, cracking open the skulls of drum fish, next to the tirelessness of ancient gar passing unseen through waters and time? A flash among the stars. But one will outlive the other. I think about the trash fish flopping, slippery in the young boy's hand. He's wide-eyed like a moccasin when the blood hits the water. Could be he's seeing into the future as he grabs that slippery, flopping thing and hurls it with his teeth clenched. He's figuring out what the world is all about.

The morning sun rose over the shoreline that rested in the water. The dirt sucked up the blood, and the entrails settled into the lake bottom to be picked at by water-bound scavengers. Texoma looked like a bowl of leftovers covered with saran wrap, the water hushed and pink with dawn. A gar's head touched the surface and the small waves spread toward the shore in all directions, merging with the flatness beyond and sweeping up my nerves, still caught up in visions of poisoned limbs and convulsing bodies. The gar broke the water once more and breathed deep, its bladder filling with moist air, as the dew dripped from the riparian grass onto the water, rousing a faint dance, a silent ballet.

After the fish fry, I lay in a hammock hanging on an oak that split right from the ground outside of the lake house. The trunk twisted and flowed into a thin crown. I was thinking about the way those snakes moved in the water and that afternoon in the pool among the gar when millennia stopped for a moment. Time seemed to slow down and speed up all at once as those snakes struck the empty air at my feet. I was at the whim of wildness and unbound to time in those moments, frozen and rapid, there was violence and fucking. They struck me the same way. That much is clear to me, though I didn't see it then.

GAIA WAS FOURTEEN WHEN HER SOUL FELL INTO THE DEEP FRYER

2 am—the knuckles rapping against my front door were attached to the scarred hands of a manic mystic. She had just finished her shift on the phone sex hotline. In her purse was a roundtrip ticket to the center of creation.

In the weeks since we'd met, Dotty stared at me unwavering despite my awkward fidgeting.

"You don't like to look people in the eyes, do you? Does it make you uncomfortable?"

"I don't know. Maybe."

Her dress billowed around her, loose and grazing her curves, emphasizing the length of her torso. The pock marks on her face and shoulders made her self-conscious, though you could only tell because she altered photos of herself, creating a projection that haunted the periphery of digital temples—Facebook, Myspace, Twitter. Through our friendship, we learned a lot about ourselves, because there was nothing to discover between us, nothing to unearth, only the two platonic non-identities that we presented to one another. We both had little to show from our explorations of self. She was eighteen, but there was an elder phantom that stuck to her spirit. She lost her mother, and she felt all along that she was coping rather than becoming, but I witnessed something working through her that I could never define in a way that would make it tangible to either of us. And I'd lost something otherworldly. I believed it was love, but it was really just a thought.

For a time, I could sense the weight of Dotty's loss like she carried her mother with her until her soul, dense and clingy, could be lifted by something other than her child. Everyone told Dotty that she looked like her mother. Everyone said she had an essence that felt like her mother's.

The knocks came as the last drops of rain fell outside and left everything more sentient. The moisture caught in the spider's web on the porch sent it scurrying. You could see her through the glass door with the decaying wood porch and the moonlight and the stone in the garden.

Joni's hair was long, flowing past his shoulders, shining with natural black and artificial blue, nearly touching the floor as he leaned back with his legs propped up over the armrest of an overstuffed chair. Joni was adopted from Fiji by a white family and was subjected to a suburban life that looked a lot like any other. Joni was a poet and a musician whose ability to freestyle was nearly supernatural, the words poured from his chest in a deluge like the peak of spring runoff. His hands sweat too much and it plagued him. Whether he was meeting someone for the first time and shaking their hand or running his fingers through a lover's, the sweat was always there. He said someday he'd move back to Fiji where the climate would dry his palms. But Joni moved to Portland instead and became something of a celebrity in the underground hip-hop scene. I watched the content of his songs change as we grew older and came to know loss in a real way.

Joni continued to read Lorca aloud as I got up and walked across the living room to unlock the door. Joni was broken-hearted too. The result of a punk girl who gave herself stick and poke tattoos and lopsided haircuts. We all felt some kinship in our shared melancholia, though Dotty's was something that neither Joni nor I could grasp then. It wizened her in a way that was beyond us. That night, Joni displayed an explosive optimism that he took on when he needed to cover his sadness.

Dotty smiled at me with her chin down. This brief acknowledgment was the only indication that she noticed me before moving past and taking her place on the green couch. I sat beside her. Her orbit smelled like lavender, and it made me think of immortality. Her hair, blonde and thin, fell down in shining, greasy clumps along the ridge of her shoulders. She dug through her oversized purse, pulled out a small baggie, shook it, and asked, "You boys ever tried DMT?" Her teeth were set into her head like comets, long and white with space between them, and her smile was devious and generous; she was saintly.

She foraged prairie mimosa, which grows on the plains and can be a source of dimethyltryptamine with a proper MAO inhibitor or used for extraction. She tossed the baggie onto the table in front of us. Joni and I were both intimidated by the thing. That's the right way to feel in the presence of one of the strongest hallucinogens on the planet. For many people, psychedelics command a great deference. I am one of these people. If you have enough psychedelic experiences, you too will inevitably be this person. Ultimately, it is for you to decide whether the bliss and the insight outweigh the horror and the confusion. Or, more to the point, if you are at ease existing within the horror and confusion. Once you have dedicated yourself to this cosmic chaos, it is important to craft the circumstances of your experience with a certain level of scrutiny, so that you don't end up curled in the corner fearing that your final few thoughts are going to be siphoned from your head like it's a goddamn slushee machine.

But we wanted to see deeper things, farther things, so that the world would open up within us or to us. We just wanted the world to open. For me, it didn't just open that night, it shattered and melted away into a billowing molecular infinity. From my chest unfurled a blanket of endless colors I had never seen before, the blanket kept pouring from within me until it covered all the world starting with the Nissan Sentra in the driveway that was crusted with puke from my roommate's drunken sickness two nights before, then over the hedges beyond, and it lifted itself above the neighbor's house, moving, coating, consuming until the world was wrapped in its technicolored cloth. Then it inhaled itself, moving back towards me from all sides until it was only a rippling carpet made from the fabric of the earth system, myself an extension of it.

And I got a sense of what the wilderness wandering Taoists meant when they said there is no inner and outer, no self and other, no material and immaterial, no sacred and no profane. The planet became me, and it was something that could not be unrealized. A tired trope of burned out street philosophy that could not be unfelt. Planetary consciousness. And all of this began to fold in on itself, the thoughts and connections informing each other from the edge of time in all directions. And everything was a spinning nebula that stretched into a vacuum the size of a pinhole. All the colors seemed to eat themselves and digest everything, excreting wild hues even more vibrant and far-reaching and smoother, free from all texture, and there were no longer feelings but a feel to everything. Cast out toward open sky from the prairies of the flyover to the space debris, and there was a jiggling cerebral silt until the final lactation, then a bath of pure white.

A voice came from beyond: "Why the fuck are you standing in the middle of the street? You're not losing your shit are you? Is this gonna be a scene? If this is gonna be a god damned scene, I'll put on my trip-sitting game-face and drag you inside, you mother fucker!" yelled Dotty, my shaman, sitting cross-legged by a tree stump, her arms extended behind her with her weight on her palms.

"No Dotty. The opposite, really. I think everything is going to be different for me now."

Joni was similarly affected, and for a long time he searched the world over to find whatever it was that came to him during the trip in the form of a talking cat, and he'll tell me to this day that he still hasn't found it. Whatever it was that reached out to him and gave him a sense of calm and a little advice that must have rang too true.

Later that night Dotty was sprawled out across the bed, staring through the darkness at the ceiling and telling me that she felt icky. She said when she was on the clock that most of the client's fantasies or roleplay didn't bother her, but then there was pedophilia and incest stuff and it made her feel like her soul was rotting. And she said it like this, her voice quietly coming from the other end of the bed, "Sometimes these men, the things they say, they get stuck in my head and I can't get them out... things about children, their daughters, violent things... I sit with it all the time, and I can't think about anything else."

"Do you have to listen to them?"

"I can't hang up. They'd fire me, because there's nothing illegal about fantasizing."

She didn't know how to cope with it, knowing that those men exist in the world. That you can see them in the produce department at your grocery store or riding bumper cars at the state fair. I kept hearing her words and her breath, and I imagined her face, expressionless except for her eyes which wanted to take hold of her blond hair, drop onto her shoulders, and roll away forever. I could almost feel the gravity of the void that would be left below her eyebrows, even through the darkness. And you could tell she wanted to move on, knowing that I had nothing to offer, though my churning stomach wished to wrench something out at that moment that could save her from all that sadness. She changed subjects without changing subjects.

"One told me that he wanted me covered in oil, and I thought he meant like lube, but he meant like actual black oil, like from the ground. And he wanted to pour it on me and use it to fuck me."

"That's weird."

"It was pretty weird."

We fell asleep with our feet in each other's faces.

I awoke to the sound of a mourning dove and lifted my head from my pillow with a stiff neck. I had slept on a bag of mugwort and dreamed about a hole in my head that I could stare down in the mirror and there was only bone and blood and brain and it scared me. Oddly enough, everything in me that morning felt the limitless nature of my senses. Outside the sun was rising, and I felt a brief warmth that came through the window behind the bed, though it was still cold outside the blankets, and I took a moment to count the shadows of the furniture in the room. The shadow of the nightstand, the shadow of the shoe rack, the shadow of the cedar box. A few moments before, I was looking straight ahead into a patch of darkness and that darkness looked like all of the darkness in the room, but I felt that it was mine, my patch of night.

Dotty's feet were still in my face, and she was sleeping heavily. I walked out to the front porch and sat in the rocking chair to catch the smell of dew and the coming rain—to feel that invigorating moisture. Once the summer drought set in, I would lose the smell of rain that kept me sprite in the early days of spring. There was the spider in its web on the handrail. I grabbed a fly, and I fed it. I watched it eat as dawn drowned out the light from the lamp on the porch, wrapped in a blanket stretched tight around my shoulders. There was static that morning, and it filled the emptiness.

Days like that one passed quickly and the moments were lost to empty spots of mind, where I drank coffee and sat with all of the promises I had made to myself and then forgotten. That morning I thought of being a kid and resting my head on a feather pillow at night, tight beneath the blanket and the comfort of the Lord floating above me. I'd imagine having entered paradise after living a righteous life, and finding that it lasts for eternity. Then, overcome with panic, I'd wish for a great escape into eternal nothing. I'd ask God if he could make it good, good enough that I'd want it to last forever. I considered it a sort of infiniphobia—fear of the infinite—but things felt different that morning and the thought of endless chaos was accompanied by a sense of ease.

There was a wet piece of paper in my hands, and I wanted to jot something down. A few words about the rain on the window that looked like a million little beads holding the clouds they came from. They traced themselves along the smooth glass, creeping under the force of gravity, while dripping freely from the roof and the leaves of the tomato plant bearing several fruit that would soon come to ripen, and making a pattering sound that came and went over the squeak of my chair and Satie.

The door opened, and I watched the mist float into the house as Dotty walked out. I turned to her with two eyes loosely connected to something resembling a brain, though it had seen too much, and I still felt like I was experiencing her in deep time, as earthworms and molecules, while she took in a great big breath of air and hung around.

Dotty had grown tired of her own desperation, and she wanted nothing more than to mean something to someone. This may not seem like a lot to ask, but some of us never see our own worth appreciated through someone else's desires. We sat outside and shared a cigarette and she looked at a red and white pattern making stars around the center of an amaryllis blossom. The flower had been there for a day, and it would be gone by Friday.

She looked at the lines in her hands, tracing her fingers over them, "Can you tell me what they mean?"

"I don't know what they mean, but I'm sure someone does."

"My hands are wrinkly and they have too many lines. They would probably overwhelm a palm reader... My brain is broken."

"Your brain seems fine to me. Anyway, your brain isn't your soul, right? They exist in, like, two different places, and they only seem to meet when everything is going really fucking well. I don't know much about souls, but I think you've got a good one."

I have to admit, the lines in her hand resembled the faults running through the hills, as her palm curved toward me and I ran my thumb over it. It felt tense and there were scars along her arms where she burned herself working over a deep fryer at fourteen.

Then the morning rain picked up and there was a grayness to the sky that lacked any sort of sinister disposition, and it brought some calm instead with the smell of life, green and effervescent. This moment would not last long, but as I looked at her hands and their lines and the misdirection therein, I cared deeply for her and I cared deeply for everything around us that made her. The open porch broke to a tall row of shrubs that contained the yard and the grass was singing in the moisture, reaching up to the horizon and hoping that it would never end.

I looked toward the Oklahoma sky, imagining it as an ocean filled with waves and the plains a sky upon which I was weightless. I danced upon the emptiness toward another day at work or to another night of drinking. Sometimes that weightlessness is there, and sometimes I feel so heavy that I could crush through the red dirt, only to get sucked up like raw oil, refined, and slurped, to make the machines of civilization turn. Everything disappears into the red again. Nothing escapes it, not even when I traveled by jumbo plane to an exotic island off the coast of Croatia to have brief moments of intimacy with a Montenegrin man who spoke perfect English. The red was always at my heels getting lapped up by the flapping mouth of my sole, which began to separate from my boot somewhere in Budapest. I went to clean it, and there was Oklahoma clay hiding along the curve of my foot.

To Dotty, the world looked like collective grief, as she floated across the plains, nothing in mind but the few sunny days that formed the backbone of her reason to keep breathing and working. She chased Sunyata to forego the burden of embodiment, because the world seemed too fucked up to feel like Self. All her glory was caught up in the well-being of someone she may never meet. She looked into the rain, "I get tingly when it rains in the morning. It's the same feeling I get when I hear the wind in the tree limbs…"

And sitting with her then, I thought of Venice with a belly full of wine at the Peggy Guggenheim Museum, believing I was more than I was while looking at the paintings of Magritte, Picasso and Pollock. I think of Pollock when I stare at asphalt. Dotty and I were waiting together, hoping to sacrifice our days until there was nothing left to send forward in time, which was moving constantly in all directions, spreading its inertia and its indifference into the cracking character of our very human agreement. The shape of existence rolled through our thoughts like wheat on the plains and we got swept into that great big cosmic combine seeing nothing but the monoculture chopped and whirling around us. We sat on the porch until the sunset pulled on the clouds and they colored themselves into our minds like a strung-out painter tap dancing across the Void, palette in hand, verbose and malnourished, and Dotty glistened looking like a benevolent Martian.

Sometime later she called and asked if my father still practiced law, which he didn't. She said she had been locked in her bathroom with a kitchen knife for five hours, because she rushed into a living situation with some abusive son of a bitch under the pressure of her homelessness.

"Things are not going well for me," she said. And there was hope in her voice.

MICROCHIMERISM

Fifteen miles east of Albuquerque, the snow began to fall. I was looking northward from the passenger seat, thinking about Chisholm Trail and those long, treacherous cattle drives that split America in two. Three miles ahead, a semi-truck carrying Tyson's mutated chicken parts was tipped over and stretched across I-40, leaving traffic at a standstill. We needed to get off at the next exit and barrel down Route-66 through Navajo country all the way to Flagstaff, where we could nestle into a couple of stiff beds until the sun came back.

I was happy to be out of the panhandle of Texas, away from the Staked Plains and into the Southwest. Wilson was uncomfortable behind the wheel, wide-eyed and staring into the great brightness that consumed the New Mexican vista, jittering with a nervousness that was just shy of neurosis as the snow built up beneath the tires of his Honda Civic. Wilson wasn't comfortable in casual conversation. When he spoke he did so with a dissociated voice, and his words tumbled over themselves, not quite matching his intentions and lingering too long in moments of silence that were meant to be filled. I met Wilson in a Chinese philosophy class where we shuffled in everyday after drinking too much whiskey. Lao Tzu and Knob Creek made for admirable bedfellows.

Mia sat in the backseat next to an ice chest filled with

beer and tuna fish. Everything in Mia grew from her fierce independence. She effortlessly faced down situations of masculinity in crisis, even if she was scared inside. She had never crossed the Oklahoma border to the west, but she had flown to New York City once with her high school choir to perform in the Macy's Thanksgiving Day Parade. Amid the snow's blinding intensity, a police officer was speeding through the median, showing off for gridlocked onlookers until his patrol car got stuck. We were lucky enough to be parked beside the spectacle and I laughed, recording video and snapping pictures as the cop struggled to push the squad car from the snowbank. We were still there when a tow truck came to pull the cruiser back onto I-40 sometime later.

I met Mia at a time when I desperately needed a friend like her. I was beginning to lose sight of any sort of ambition. I came across too much in the ways of thievery and neophyte hustling, and, never overly fond of schoolwork to begin with, I let my studies fall to the wayside in favor of niche psychedelics and bohemian delusions. Mia transferred from a community college in Tulsa, deciding to take on a lifetime of debt and pursue an underappreciated career as a high school teacher. Having dealt with a life of economic insecurity, being the poor girl at a rich high school, she felt she could bring the spark of intellectual fervor to bored, meme-saturated students. She struggled with addiction, having spent the better part of her early teens taking to the ecstatic pleasure of huffing keyboard cleaner. The realization that she may be caught in the grips of addiction hit her after she spent a week scratching at the Adam's apple she believed was growing in her throat. Otherwise confident in her feminine allure, she thought she could be transforming into a man. She went to rehab after her parents found sixty empty aerosol cans under the daybed in the spare bedroom.

The asphalt below connected us from sea to sea, as the US interstate system rolled out in all directions, creating a vast web, veins cracking and steaming across the body of

America. I-40 in particular runs from Barstow, California to Wilmington, North Carolina, winding through America's empty progressive promises to its ever-present history of racial brutality. We sunk into the acceptance that the weather was going to set our trip a day behind. We had every intention of getting to the Grand Canyon that night, but Flagstaff was the best we could do.

The night was thick in northern Arizona. We pulled into a motel painted with a desert panorama, bright reds and blues depicted a sunset spreading behind a saguaro cactus. Mia told the late-night clerk she was alone, and they only charged us for one person. By the time morning came, there was a new attendant at the desk, and they were none the wiser. I stepped outside to find the motel was built snugly into a rock face that rose straight into empty skies. They were bright blue without any sense of longing for those clouds that followed us the day before.

Mia stepped into the sun with big sunglasses and a wide brimmed hat that cast shade all the way down to her chest.

"Let's get out of here. I'm ready to see this fucking canyon."

It was only an hour and a half drive through the misted, desert morning. The time in the car felt short and we were rejuvenated looking forward at the changing landscape that came to bear some trees, white fir and blue spruce.

The rangers pointed us to the designated campsites and said they were open, but they were buried in snow. We were the only people at the campground that morning, but folks flocked in as the days went on and the slippery, sticky white that covered the ground melted into a slippery, sticky red. The snow was packed to our knees, and we dug with shovels and sticks to put up a tent and build a fire circle. After home base was built we went to find the canyon and got lost walking through the woods, getting caught in a thick stand of serviceberry that we pushed through until it opened to a ledge from which we saw only a jagged expanse rolling over into its shadows, layers of geology climbing motionless toward the drop in front of us, and for the first time in my life all that I could see was wild. I felt nothing but the landscape's emptiness, and I felt empty too. It was an emptiness that did not need to be filled. I identified with the dirt, red and cascading, and I was overcome with an appreciation for the red that was at the foundation of my being. Without any clear definition there was only an obscured frontier of self, lifted between the canyon and the sky before me, and I laughed. Mia laughed. Wilson laughed. And our laughter defined the moment.

Some years later Wilson went to prison for running a clandestine chemistry lab where he extracted large quantities of dimethyltryptamine. I thought he was performing a community service, but the law considered it a felony drug conviction. The cops caught wind of it by way of a dry snitch who took it upon himself to spread the good news as one is tempted to do after moments of profound insight. The night the cops raided Wilson's duplex has become something of a legend as there were various local celebrities present—professors, musicians, and artists. The bust was the talk of the town, though everyone told the story differently. People act desperate under the threat of legal repercussions or due to the deceit of cops salivating at the thought of dragging in a drug charge. Wilson was doing well in school then, but the raid happened and that changed things and he was never quite the same. His life was upended and he moved back to Tulsa to live with his dad, working at a moving company and spending his evenings with Evan Williams, scouring the underbelly of red-pilled internet forums.

The next morning, we awoke to the sound of snow collapsing and compacting beneath the hooves of a bull elk. It was a stretching hollow sound that floated beneath the limbs of the ponderosas outside of our tent. We made a morning fire and instant coffee. The smell of juniper smoke in the morning filled me with an odd sense that my mind was outside of my skull and exploring things on its own. At dawn, the canyon was defined by a deep darkness that swallowed sight and was distended like an empty stomach into the fading stars of the night sky. As the sun rose, the sky reflected the slick rock upon which it shed its light, only it was glowing and forcing itself into every corner that still held night. To find a source of life-affirming reverie in the sight of the sun rising over the stone lips of the Grand Canyon is easy. The ground was indistinguishable from the sky as the darkness dissipated to reveal the red hidden inside of it. A condor flew overhead, its 12-foot wings stretched across the great shadow of the canyon that morning, and we walked in the dark until the blackness was broken in counted rays.

Lao Tsu wrote that a thing's use comes from its emptiness, like a cup or a window, the space between your thoughts or wildness and canyons that appear to lumber on elbows and knees up a ladder toward infinite sky. And I was floating in that space then, between swollen thoughts as we hit the Kaibab trail and descended into the emptiness, chewing ephedra while the horse flies chewed through me, as if they believed the heat had taken me already—just a sack of organs bubbling beneath the Arizona sun. And there were thin-framed French runners sprinting directly down the side of the canyon. Quite literally straight down it, right through the "Do not walk" areas between the switchbacks. It felt like I had legs that I couldn't see to carry me, floating, despite the snow and the heat rising from the dirt in the canyon below us. The red swirled in wild patterns obscured by the heat, though the top of the canyon was still covered with several inches of snow, and the snow too was being picked up by the wind, lifted into the sky, appearing as a crystallized dust settling from the collapse of a dying star.

Mia lost her footing and came toward me with the forces of gravity and panic propelling her. She was screaming, flailing, trying to stop herself as the ice took her closer and closer toward a drop that meant her death. Then the moment came when she was going to barrel through me, and I weighed my options, seeing her frenzied form moving toward me like that. Should I square up, sink my yak-traks into the solid ice, and try to stop her? I'm no hero. I flattened myself against the canyon wall, sucking in my gut and letting her glide past with no indication that she'd slow down before soaring into the mouth of the canyon. If she did survive, I was certain she'd forgive me, because a mutual interest in self-preservation and a love for living had always forged our bond. The ledge got closer, and I thought of the red of her insides mixing with the red dirt, the helicopter ride with Mia's shattered corpse, the guilt that would follow, and more than anything, the world without her whooping and hollering, stony-eyed certainty. I watched as she slid within five feet of the drop, finally slowing and coming to a stop.

"What the fuck was that?" She yelled, breathing heavy, "I just almost fucking died. God damn ice almost blasted me right out the Kaibab. Holy shit."

I moved down to help her up. She would talk about this moment for years to come, both the brush with death, and my failure to act.

Looking out over the colossal, snaking hole, I couldn't spin the story any tighter through my mind. The surface of the canyon walls, its coarseness heaving and running from the valley into the mending of the river with the horizon, itself a notch upon the landscape. The erosion of the earthen face over time as the Colorado chewed through the stone—millennia the water spent grazing with patience and dexterity upon the sandstone and granite, pouring itself back into the Gulf of California. And I watch that erosion swallowed by the water and resting to make the riverbed where the walleye chew at the detritus and the rolling boulders give the water its oxygen. But the dam went in, and for most of my life, the Colorado has not fed the Gulf of California as it had for millions of years, and instead is consumed over the course of its travels by farmers, ranchers, municipalities, and industrialists. As a matter of fact, as I looked out over that wild running river, it was going to dry out somewhere in Arizona before it reached the Mexican border.

I have only known rivers interfered with, rivers given false names. The Oklahoma River runs a few miles through the City, but outside of that it's commonly referred to as the Canadian. Not far from the Oklahoma River you'll find I-40, the highway that brought us west only a few days before. On the Skydance Bridge that stretches across that highway, there is a sculpture of a scissor-tailed flycatcher straddling eight lanes of traffic, but it's pretty abstract. If you are speeding through you might look at it without realizing it's a bird, but rather some Dadaist industrial architecture welded in bizarre patterns like an oversized jack that fell from the clouds and got stuck on the overpass.

A mile or two from the bridge, a canal runs through downtown Oklahoma City, diverted from the Oklahoma River so people can shop and drink beer at Hooters right next to the water, close to nature. There are apartment buildings that line the streets of the Deep Deuce neighborhood nearby. There were once holes in the walls of those apartments where you could stick your arm in holding a sweaty ball of cash and someone on the other side would heat a spoon and feed you a syringe of opiates or amphetamines—they called it the shooting gallery. Now you walk by those same apartments, and there are Bradford pears blooming over freshly watered grass, and you can grab a baguette or a steak. The remodel displaced the addicts, and they were left to find new places to die out of sight. The drugs are still there, but they've been repackaged in pill form to suit corporate offices for the professional-managerial class who came to serve the beneficiaries of the second big oil boom that took place after fracking became popular practice. In the morning, the streets of Deep Deuce are quiet, resting on the periphery of downtown, and you can find some peace there while everything still moves but you hear none of it. When the wings of the flies are louder than the turning wheels of the police cars and a calm rests within you, the corruption lies just beyond earshot. The trees remind me of the forest that once surrounded my parents' home, before all my fears played out despite my soft defiance. The trees in the city move, catching wind like the oaks in the forest, and if you stare into their branches for a while you may see the same song flowing from them, the world turning through the heartwood. And some part of your sterile lust for something more wild than your apartment courtyard sweeps through you but you swat it away and sip your coffee letting the taste fill your throat, the warmth permeating through your belly, before you make your way to the office.

I sat on the trunk of a dead cottonwood near the canyon's edge eating orange slices and looking out into all of the incarnations of red, the structures of Earth rising like a sandcastle built over eons, shaped by the hands of water. I think of civilization with its big, swinging gait knocking it all down, then the material reincorporated into the swirling pieces of slow-moving things. Maybe civilization is feeble despite its capacity to end it all. The land around the Grand Canyon could be opened to *energy exploration*, and I wonder what all of this wild would look like then, pushed even further out of sight. A vulture wobbled in front of the sun as it pushed through the breeze that had picked up in the last ten minutes, and it blew just right, so that I could feel the chill of the juice dripping through my fingers.

At camp, we drank merlot around the fire and smoked pot through an ambrosia apple, looking at constellations that rested beyond the light pollution we'd grown accustomed to. We were tired and dirty and overcoming a sort of blindness. The flames jerked frantically inside a circle of stones we collected while digging through the snow of the campsite.

Mia was staring into the fire when she said, "I was at the plasma center last week and they told me I'm not a viable donor anymore. They said I've been pregnant before. Must have been with that coked-up, married son-of-a-bitch. He never was honest with me, you know. Don't know why I expected him to be, seeing as the whole thing was an affair... leaving his wife and kid alone in that apartment the way he did... I know y'all didn't think much of it, but it was the most I've ever felt for anyone. So fuck you, because there was passion there. Fuck it, I'll say it, I was in love with him..."

She moved the logs on the fire and the flames rose. She wasn't crying. She saved that for moments alone. But she wasn't feeling right and you could see it.

"They said that cells from the baby are still in my blood, and they'll be there forever causing health issues and shit. Something called microchimerism. If I get pregnant in the future, which I'd like to, then the baby will be at risk of getting attacked by the cells from the kid that miscarried. Even after the baby is born those cells will still be there, and it could cause that kid some health problems. Poor little bastard."

Mia looked up into the night and there was a red from the fire held in her eyes like she saw through the darkness, reflecting the rollicking canyon hidden beyond the trees and their shadows, and she let out a heavy breath, turning her gaze toward the constellations. She was within all of it.

"Anyway, it's going to be a real pain in the ass trying to figure out what to do without that extra 200 bucks a month. Seven-fifteen an hour just doesn't cut it. A girl's gotta eat, you know?"

We watched the sunrise again and had no plans for the day, so Wilson and I hiked down Bright Angel trail. Mia didn't want to go back into the canyon, so she stayed at camp and explored the edge with a group of tourists standing on a glass platform that was suspended above the chasm.

At Bright Angel trailhead, the snow melted and there was thawing mule shit along the path from the pack tours that went down before us. Wilson didn't say much. He could be quiet at times, and he was focused as we made our way down.

There was a slight breeze that I could feel through my sweat-shirt. I had a tuna sandwich smashed in a ziplock bag. The chollas became abundant and the trail flattened, opening in an expanse where we stopped to rest.

I sat with Wilson and his silence. A silence that could have been one of reflection or annoyance or maybe he just didn't have anything to say. I didn't care to dissect the moment. I let him have it, and we rested there with the wind blowing through us and through the chollas, carrying dried mustard grass through the emptiness of the canyon. And we observed it with a humble fascination as we went deeper and the canyon devoured everything. It consumed us like a cluster of cells floating through the caverns of the Southwest, red and swallowing it all. We were at once awestruck and angry, because we were not allowed a future filled with wildness and dreams and balance. It's not something that either of us needed to say.

The heart of the Southwest is dry and dusty, but it teems with life that moves as you piss in the presence of hoodoos, the web of stars above pulsing so bright there seems to be an interstellar glow connecting the lightyears between them. Everything we held in us (and it wasn't much) was picked up in the sprawl of that canyon, the layers of geology born from time in numbers that we could not grasp being so small but caught in a great cascade of rocks and emptiness pushing in all directions, ladders to the trap door of our dreams, and though the moment was already gone, it seemed inescapable. The desert stretches on either side of us, with a permanence unknown to the world around it. In stillness, it is prepared for what lies ahead, becoming more attuned with itself, with its moments of adapted life scurrying across the sand where the water licks the dust only to disappear bent into its own purgatory.

We ran out of breath on the way back up and asked someone to take our photo below a stone arch. I keep that picture saved and I look at it sometimes. We appeared to be propped up by a crooked certainty, and I still don't know if it was a certainty of our place in the world or just lost wonder.

Mia and I yelled at each other in a parking lot, because she wanted to watch the sunset and I was exhausted and wanted to go back to camp. Had the sky broken open and delivered some undeniable sign from God, we would have written it off as a shift in the afternoon clouds. We learned nothing and that was okay. Back then, we just needed to see something we believed was wild.

When the gift shop at the end of the parking lot closed, there was a woman sitting on the curb crying. The sun set behind her. The light on her form was casting shadows into the wrinkles of her face and then the sun went down behind the canyon and she disappeared. A street lamp flickered on in the parking lot. It was yellow and dim. It lit up the asphalt and the white lines of the handicap spot below it. When the darkness vanished, the woman was still gone.

The rest of the trip passed quickly the way they always do. No matter where I'm at, time gets away from me, and the days seem like a long trip that'll be behind me soon. Age and time, the brevity of it all sticks to my nerves as does the endlessness. I moved around in the driver's seat sitting with my own dropped jaw, as the sky took on oranges and pinks that pushed upon one another. The gear shift gave a little resistance as I dropped it into third and pulled off the highway into the parking lot of a Phillips 66. Inside, there was a wall of potato chips with a hundred different flavors. I stood and stared for what felt like hours.

THE PHENOMENOLOGY
OF BAD SEX

Ruby had Oklahoma's red dirt in her. She grew from the clay and manganese, and there was no future in which she would leave it. Her hair was the color of dusty strawberries, pale because they hadn't ripened yet. She was short, and she exploded from the ground when she moved, wading through smoke and touchy hands with a deliberateness reserved for those who had lived too hard too young. There was always a subtle, focused intensity beneath her bloodshot eyes. Ruby spun circles around me, because I was younger and less experienced in the ways of hedonism. She was the walls of a temple built for Dionysus. She fell back into herself in a way that was only fitting for someone entirely sure of their ability to decipher right from wrong. She carried all the weight of her own morality but remained remarkably nimble as she traipsed through situations of oblivion. It was this confidence that made her irresistible to anyone pulled in by the gravity of her bad posture and her earthy cadence. I was no different.

I held on to my virginity for longer than I should have. It is a mistake I'd warn against, as it drowns the joy of the first sexual experience in a pool of expectation, consisting more likely of brief, ill-considered spasms followed by a rush of anxiety, especially if it happens between the legs of someone more erotically sophisticated than yourself.

So Ruby came along with her hair like dusty fruit, and a

sexual yearning that poured from her body language as she worked her way over to the couch with a blunt hanging from her mouth and said, "Scoot over." I moved and she sat herself beside me, and before I knew it weeks had passed and she was under the covers asking to take the virginity I'd been cherishing. I was ready to put it behind me, so I did. The situation unfurled how I imagined it would—a quick, ecstatic explosion followed by shame and an apology. She said it was fine, but I could sense her disappointment. After the moment was over and I finally felt the relief of a squandered sexual purity, we went out for pizza. I looked at her across the table, over a pitcher of beer. Her chin was rounded like a bowling pin, her neck thin, and the only thing I could see was a vague boredom inside of her.

Prior to meeting Ruby, I was lucky enough to feel young love for an introverted girl named Olivia. But I was never able to overcome the sprawl of her sadness because I couldn't see it through my bliss. After she broke things off, I glimpsed her in numbers and inanimate objects, everything reminded me of her, and I held fast to the belief that she would come to her senses. In turn, I allowed myself to become wrapped up in her vague romantic gestures. Her favorite color was green. That fact is insignificant, and it doesn't figure into my understanding of the plains or the mountains in any real way. It's the timid sexuality that resulted from that relationship that is significant. The way I feared my body. In those days, she populated my dreams in the subconscious where the wild still prevails.

Psychoanalyst Wilhelm Reich called sexual repression a *chronic biopathy of the organism* when addressing the mass psychology of fascism. Reich believed that this could be considered a contributing factor to human domestication. We deny our inherent sensuality and that has led to a belief that human nature is distinct from a planet in which we are otherwise ecologically enmeshed.

When it came to Olivia, there was never any sense that things would work out for us. Every indication was that things would carry on as they always had only slightly worse, and as such it was an acute meditation on the evolution of human progress. There was something about her disinterest that was haunting like sounds from space as we grew older and gave ourselves to others, toiling toward a thought that existed in decades passed with no recollection of our broken promises or the hollow mannequins we built of one another.

Around her, the earth moved in patterns, eating its own darkness and feeding into the curves in the small of her back. I could see the way her dark hair pulled itself from the shadows of the monkey grass as we sat cross legged in her mother's garden fingering the wood mulch. The things that shaped her rested in the flesh of the green planet. They were a product of light and rain, bridging the underworld with the heavens, so to speak, and this complexity bounced up and down on her heaving chest when her anxiety ramped up. I saw her as possessing a mind like the pando tree flowing from one thought to the next, tumbling over the emptiness that characterized the objects around her, and she never seemed to notice it.

She had thick hair, black with a coarse volume, that grew in dense stands along her arms, and for years it made her self-conscious, so she shaved it. As age carried her, or lifted her rather, into a supreme self-confidence and she grew from a lanky awkward teenager into a young woman, often the object of carnal thoughts, a sort of right hand to the tyranny of lust, she let her hair grow thick on the olive complexion of her arms and it, as a testament to her confidence, became another mark of her beauty.

What can I say about the way we betrayed our intuitions or the denial that seeped from our inability to confront the ending? Honestly, I haven't thought about it much. And really, what were we going to do? Never feel such things? Sometimes it's easy. There is nothing more to say and you just walk. Other times you are tethered to a thing for years only to find that one day you let go with no particular break or severance, because all the breaking and severing has already been done, and the thing just floats away into the sun, so you can't ever look at it for too long. You keep on walking with the same brokenness you'd been carrying around for years. The source of it all having flown the roost, and you barely notice its absence, because there was grave inaction in the face of calamity.

That's how it went when Olivia left. I'd been empty for years, left to fill my trenches with ecstatic urges, and she'd found love or something like it. The kids and the dog were to come, and she seemed satisfied with it all. I don't doubt that Olivia felt a strong emotion for me, not love, but something just as illusory and fleeting—security. It was perhaps dually driven by her fascination with my veneer of freedom, though I was equally vulnerable to the web of judgment presented by most social situations, I fostered a confident demeanor that was more an amalgamation of literary personae and went on to poison my brain in ways that are still irreconcilable and spawned, for lack of a better word, my identity.

In my last memory of her, she stood in front of me, stolid and bent in the window light, with nothing much to say though you could see her mind moving toward the door into the freedom of that mucky summer night. It could have been an anxiety that leapt from the seams of what she, in a familiar tone of self-deprecation, called her *daddy issues*, which came about after she heard a voicemail on his phone from a working girl, one I imagined wore long furs and spoke only in whispers. Realistically, she had some cause for concern, whether the madness of my lust was guided toward the waiting thighs of another person or not. It was never really the sex that pulled me into strange beds. The sex felt repetitive and I was never much good at it. Instead, it was that electricity—the lack of familiarity with a new body, a new mind. The thrill of the chase ran through all my attempts at fidelity. There are acts of infidelity more intimate than one night stands, emotional infidelities. Monogamy, as it turns out, is not for the young.

But we ran together for years as budding kids who soon became very different adults that neither one of us had much interest in, though this was difficult to admit to one another, and it took us the better part of ten years to sort out the confusion. In our early teens, we built a mythology around each other's virginity, growing out of the puritanism of the bible belt, and it was a stowaway on my sexual voyage for years. No one bothered to tell me that there is no such thing as virginity, so I continued to guard that myth. It occurs to me that I must have been waiting for her. Thinking that it was destined that we consummate our delusions, because I quickly found Ruby and relieved myself of the burden after being informed that Olivia had done the same.

It was through these experiences that I came to know my body and hold it in contempt. I abused it because I felt it had imprisoned me. I was alienated from the very thing that allowed me to explore the world. And this only further distanced me from recognizing the expanse of my *flesh* as I understand it now.

We only fucked once before Ruby told me the relationship wasn't working and left me to sit with that embarrassment. Now, looking back on these events of a decade ago, I can't remember if she bothered to see me. Perhaps it was a phone call or a text. It doesn't matter. I knew that I couldn't hold onto her. It wasn't what either of us wanted or needed. I needed to be relieved of a burden and she wanted nothing more than to do that for me. That was it. She said she ran into her ex at a party and there were lingering feelings that she needed to act upon. He was an outlaw and a bull rider, fueled by Wild Turkey.

A dusty green dildo stood on my windowsill behind the bamboo blinds. It was translucent green and beyond it, through the window, trees broke the sunlight into odd patterns refracted by the ribbed texture of the sex toy. I picked it up, running my fingers through the dust. I thought of Lyme disease. I recalled feeling love for the first time after losing it and how quickly that love left and an empty feeling rose again. The dildo reminded me of a tree trunk that I saw once in the forest around my family's house. It was hollowed, decomposing, and the whole thing, inside and out, was covered with vibrant green moss. We used that dildo once when it was still flopping and luminous, and I was too drunk to get hard. Abigail asked if there was something wrong with her. I said no. She pulled that dildo from the drawer on the bedside table and the green disappeared inside of her.

Joni's apartment felt off, because a bounty hunter claiming to be Amir's uncle had pushed through the front door two days before. Amir was Joni's roommate, and he was asleep upstairs when the bounty hunter pulled him from his bed and dragged him down the stairs by his ankles for skipping court on a marijuana charge. I was sleeping on the couch when I heard the commotion. Thinking it was the police, I hid a bag of Mexican red hair under the sink with a bong and a grinder.

I'd been in some trouble at Joni's too. After getting locked outside and almost pissing myself, I found a dark corner under a stoop to relieve the sharp pain in my bladder, but the police were patrolling the parking lot and put a spotlight on my dick, citing me with something called Outraging Public Decency. I disagreed with that charge on every account. There was no public. No one was outraged, and there is nothing indecent about the demands of the body.

After all that went down, everyone sat uncomfortably in the living room grappling with awkward bouts of silence and an unbending tension. Abigail and I decided to get far away from the vexed energy whirling around in the days since Amir's arrest and all the uneasiness that came with it. We hopped in the Jeep just before sunset and headed south to the Wichita Wildlife Refuge.

The sun was setting, getting sucked into the horizon, gripping the sky with fingers of light, thin and spread wide to keep itself from being engulfed. It spanned the extent of a land that was bare and unbroken against the asphalt, sucking up the empty beyond. There was macaroni and weed in the backseat for the highness and the hunger that would follow. Abigail read to me as I sped down the highway to the wildlife preserve where there was one hill we called a mountain and herds of buffalo that look like haggard shamans. Night came and the tunneling highway channeled my attention in a hypnotic siphon, spinning to her voice as she read André Breton. Twilight was intoxicating. It felt like we were characters in a story being written from the future.

Before I'd ever read his work, Breton came to me in a dream. Maybe I'd come across his name, but I had no recollection of it. In the dream, salty water poured through the gunmetal walls of an underground bunker. Inside the bunker, military experiments were carried out in secrecy. Breton loomed as a shadow, a specter, as we tried and failed to launch his submarine. The submarine rested in front of a large hatch where we'd push it into the water, but it only floated to the ocean's surface and the whole thing started over. I woke up in the middle of the night, and promptly flipped on my bedside lamp to write down that name—André Breton. The next morning, I went to the library and searched the catalog. It was cloudy, and the rain caught me by surprise as I cut through an alley in front of a line of bolt-locked, rusted doors. I pulled several of his books from the shelf, thumbing through them on an oversized couch hidden on the third floor of the Bizzell Memorial Library, which looked like a gothic castle built from the red dirt of the southern plains. It was filled with imagery of submarines, and it read as if his words traveled through water as he wrote them. I checked out every one of Breton's books. After I finished, I read Tristan Tzara, Phillipe Soupault, and Francis Picabia, and then Guy Debord and the

Situationists who introduced me to the ideas of spectacle and psychogeography.

I met Abigail in this surreal haze of automatic writing experiments and hash brownies. The night we met, a broken boredom prodded us. We needed to do something other than sit in our friend's house slapping cockroaches from the furniture, waiting for the night to end. And we did; we went for a long, twisting walk. We were young, idealistic radicals then. She spoke openly and eloquently about her sexual forays. Orgies and strap-ons and the co-mingling of astral bodies. I asked if she had read Emma Goldman and she said "Oh, you silly boy."

Lying in bed on cool mornings with the window open, I still think of Abigail, though we were much more intoxicated then, greeting each day with vodkas before I stumbled off to my Post-Colonial Lit class. I saw her wandering through campus, her hair with so many waves it could travel through dimensions. I found it in my bed and on my clothes for months after she left. She said that I smelled like sweet dirt and no one else smelled like I did. It made me feel good, because that is who I wanted to be, a part of the earth like my grandfather. It was brief, whatever it was. Love maybe. I don't know. They say that love is everlasting like mistakes and Styrofoam, but this wasn't. It was a moment we believed we could hold onto forever. There was nothing like that in store for us. We were twenty-two and didn't breathe in life that way.

She looked out the window of the car and slipped into some state of mind that, from the position of her brow, seemed to be a deep consideration of new feelings. I ran my eyes over her face. It was chubby and her nose was round and her lips were full and her mouth was wide, but she had good, strong teeth, so the big hole in her face made her features more seductive, like they were embellished at the hands of some cosmic virtuoso, and her wild curling hair fell around it all. My fingers would get stuck in it, the hair that I found around the house after she came barreling through the door in the middle of the night screaming, "Who is the blonde?! I had a dream about a blonde! I know you're seeing one!"

I told her that there was no blonde. I was lying, but the interactions with the blonde never went beyond flirtatious phone calls. Anyway, Abigail and I had broken things off. But it was not a clean break. There were hook-ups on nights when we were drunk and lonely, then a few short-sighted expressions of regret before we finally put it all to rest.

"I think I love you, and I don't know why. I told Ester and Nicky and they don't get it either." She sat the book down on the middle console. "The whole thing is kinda weird to me. I knew I wanted you, and I get what I want, but now I feel like I'm not in control, and I'm uncomfortable with that."

I didn't understand it, because she was smarter and more mature than me. I hadn't pinned down the transient way of human emotion, though it was something I'd dealt with for years with Olivia. Once I noted it, I recognized the grift all around me. Everyone seemed to be in an unhappy relationship. They'd all abuse each other in one way or another, because they believed that the thing they were in was supposed to last forever.

Abigail continued to look at me curiously.

"Should I pull over? You could just stare at me... maybe deep into my eyes. Then it might click, you know, why you love me," I said.

"God no, if I stare at you too long, I probably won't love you anymore. Just drive the fucking car."

When we arrived at the wilderness retreat, Camp Doris was already locked up for the night. In the headlights, a rusted *Closed* sign hung crooked from the steel gate blocking the road, and there was a long, padlocked chain twisting around the bars. We suspected that this would be the case but hoped to get a site and square things up in the morning. There was a parking lot several miles back where we pulled over, laid down the seats, and rolled out a sleeping bag across the back of the Jeep. I stood out in the night under a new moon and was engrossed in darkness. There was silence. Whatever wild was beyond the parking lot felt like a dormant womb. I wondered what was out there in the black quiet. Things moving without any recognition. The ecological clockwork that ticks in unseen continuums like dreams.

Some time went by, and I was entering what promised to be a restful sleep. Then there was a knock on the window—heavy, menacing. I looked out to see a man in green. Stick pig—a ranger. We were loaded down with pot and vodka and macaroni, a cached pipe in the passenger side door. My head shot from the sleeping bag, and I wiped slobber from my chin, smearing it across my cheek. I rolled from the car and morning was cold on my face.

The sun crept over the hills of southern Oklahoma, meeting all of the defiant shapes cast from the rolling landscape and the ancient buffalo that held fast to the soil, taking slow strides through the high yellow grass. The light had a face of its own spreading across the valley and pushing the hills skyward as if awakening from a long sleep and yawning. Mount Scott peered over the shoulders of the ranger. The sky around the peak still had some night to it. There were ravens in the trees. I could see them lifting their wings when the ranger swayed.

The all-encompassing darkness that held both a feeling of empty and a cryptic sentience was dissipating, but the last moments of night endured like morning was shining through long, sleepy eyelashes. And it was. But things were moving, communicating and feeding, even throughout the night, the wild unfurled beyond my notice. The land in Oklahoma is awakening too along fault lines that were once dormant. Behind the ranger, there are old mountains, if you can call them that. They have long passed that age of chaotic friction that makes young mountains rise, but the ingenuity of empire and civilization is making old things wake up.

"Can I help you sir... er, officer?"

"You know you're not supposed to be sleeping here right?"

"No sir, guess I didn't know that. Got in pretty late last night. Had every intention of going cross the way to Camp Doris. Got in late like I said, and it turns out they got the gate closed. Place was locked up with chains. Didn't have much choice but to sleep here, sir."

"Yeah, they close up the gates around 10 pm."

"There you go. We are more than happy to pay a camping fee for last night, if that's the issue."

"Yeah, tell them you slept out here and you'd like to pay for the next two nights."

"Sure thing."

"You got your license and registration?"

"I do."

While I was fishing through the glove compartment, Abigail stepped out of the backseat and made conversation with the ranger.

"I sure wish we had known. We thought there might be a place to pay after hours. Something like those parking lots in Dallas, you know the ones?"

"Yes ma'am, that would make sense."

"Maybe I could write up a suggestion. What do you think? I could leave it in the suggestion box. Y'all have a suggestion box?"

"Not sure if they have a suggestion box. I bet if you tell Allison at the front, she could pass the word on."

"That sure would be nice. It's Allison you say?"

"Yes ma'am, Allison is the only one who works there on the weekend."

"Oh good, I'll tell Allison then."

Abigail stood nearly shoulder to shoulder with the ranger. She wore a pastel colored cotton dress. When she spoke to you, you felt free. She could make an entire room revolve around her in minutes, and there was no maliciousness to it, just a loving influence that arose inside you not through coercion but intrigue. The ranger was caught up in her honey.

My eyes were adjusting. I hadn't fished out my glasses.

The flatness that ran through the valley was still a blob surrendering itself to mild intrusions from the grass-covered hills. I fumbled through the compartment on the seatback until I found my glasses, shoving them onto my face. I saw the prairie dogs then running in the field, spinning up manic air to be breathed in by elk and white-tail deer, all of it lifted in a deranged and frenzied balance.

To the north, Rainy Mountain. It stands alone on the periphery of the Wichita range. Rainy Mountain is a holy place, home to the ancestral spirits of Kiowa that settled away from the colonizers and their genocide. Under the eyes of that great mountain, the last Sun Dance was carried out in praise of Tai-me and Talyi-da-i; beings that hold a power unseen by white settlers. But also unseen is the brutality that drove the boundaries of our frontier, creating a vision for an America regenerated through violence. They can push that history into the depth of our collective consciousness, but it remains there in the dark. It doesn't go away. It lingers in the far reaches of mind and in the reality we fabricate. Oklahoma exists near the breach that separates us from those despondent truths. It can be glimpsed from time to time. You can feel that history in the shadows of the political tempest, and it rests within Oklahoma's geographic psyche. Yes, to the north—Rainy Mountain.

I stood in front of the ranger and dawn in my underwear with a white tank top on. I'd forgotten about the pipe in the passenger door, so I pulled it open as if there was nothing criminal about it. The sun rose over those mountains eaten by time, and the shadows' banishment fully revealed the buffalo grazing at their feet and stepping lazily across the flat ground that breathed life into those hills. The buffalo reflected the illumination of morning. They were ancient and of the plains, tangling with serenity and ruin. As for me, I was trying to bend over just right to hide my misdemeanor. I opened the glove compartment and riffled through receipts and a Pike Pass and some melted gum, finally digging out the insurance verification while being sieged by anxiety, thinking at any moment this public servant would ask me to step away and give me the what-for concerning the drug laws in the land of the free while shoving me into the back of that shiny, new, tax-payer funded SUV. But it doesn't happen this time. I pulled the insurance verification out and gently closed the door so as not to send the fragile glass pipe shattering over the asphalt.

He half-heartedly looked over the documents as he continued his chat with Abigail and they chuckled and he scratched behind his ear.

"Well, I guess Doris may not be open yet. If you follow me down there, I could unlock the gate for you, so long as you promise to pay once Allison gets there."

"Sure, officer. That's no problem at all. You sure are a life-saver," said Abigail, fluttering her eyes.

That afternoon, after paying Allison, we drank pink wine and napped naked in our tent. I awoke to some noise coming from the back of the car. In our drunken idleness, we'd forgotten to close the hatch. I pulled on my pants, unzipped the tent and walked toward the car. The evening held a mild warmth. As I got closer to the vehicle, I saw that the noise was coming from a couple of raccoons turning the Jeep upside down. They'd cleared half a pan of mac-n-cheese. My primary concern was that our food was eaten. The fact that there were raccoons in the back of the Jeep seemed peripheral.

One raccoon ran off as I approached, but the other was braver, pulling its head from the fifth layer of pasta to stare at me. I stared back. There is a deep sublimity found in the pits of a raccoon's eyes. You scry and see emptiness, glimpsing into a netherworld that connects all things like a trash-eating node on Indra's web. A negative universality is held there. In a way, it is a lot like staring into the Grand Canyon. The only fitting response is to laugh and let it echo through the void. I guess when the emptiness comes crashing down on top of you as it is prone to do, you realize that the only thing that can ease the anxiety of contacting that infinite nothing is the playfulness, the laughter, the weightlessness. I picked up a hiking pole and threatened it, yelling "Git, git. Get outta here! Heyah!" It stared for a moment, tilting its head in confusion and defiance. I gave it a gentle poke. It snarled. I moved further to the side, giving it space, and it leapt from the back of the Jeep. The raccoon locked eyes with me one last time before turning away and escaping into the security of the oaks and sycamores beyond.

That night we fucked on an air mattress that deflated beneath us. There was a moaning sound rising from the trees. Then a chorus of howling coyotes rose from the underbrush, feeding the lust. Perhaps they sensed the erotic force filling the tent, pouring into night under that slight crescent moon. I felt a primal web undulating, pulsing between our bodies, and we were connected at that moment to the things moving in the darkness. There came an ecoerotic cohesion—the coyotes howling and the wind moving the leaves, causing a chill on the sweat of our bodies and the moisture rising from the dirt, soaking through the ground cover and beading up on the fabric of the tent. It was all a part of this sensual moment.

My weight has always yo-yoed, likely due to bad genetics and beer, as I am not a particularly sedentary person, possessing the odd combination of being both chubby and wiry. I have spent the majority of my adult life as a vegetarian, and I try to eat healthy, though I allow myself the occasional junk food binge on lazy weekends when the rain is falling and I have nowhere to be, usually rich caramel ice cream and alfredo pasta, filling my stomach until I'm uncomfortable. I'd have taken on bulimia if the act of self-inducing vomit hadn't been so difficult. I'd slide my fingers down my throat so my uvula was resting between my knuckles. I'd gag and cough up thick saliva but I couldn't make myself puke. Instead I've taken on a life of rapid and consistent weight fluctuation. I've struggled against my body for as long as I can remember.

It wasn't only my weight. It was my eyes too, which required strong prescriptions and thick corrective lenses to render the world around me visible. Until the age of 10 or so all the world was coagulated, a blur of everything it was supposed to be. Then one day I put on a pair of glasses and the parts of the whole became distinguishable—all the leaves of the trees and blades of grass. A similar sensation took me once the disdain I held for my body lifted and I could, if only momentarily, see things as they could be rather than as they were.

It is interesting to carry yourself through the world in different bodies every few years, gauging the way people interact with you based on your appearance. I don't judge those that are drawn to a particular body-type. I have met plenty of people who hung all over me when I was in one of my slimmer forms, only to re-emphasize how great of a friend I was when I let myself go a bit. Of course, there were chubby-chasers as well, and more often than not they were pretty people who had no interest in me outside of that fetish, but I accepted the circumstances for what they were, and I indulged them— if not for them, then for my own self-loathing brand of hedonism.

But being with Abigail was the first time I felt desired completely. I felt sure of myself and sure of the fact that her interest in me was something real and lasting. There is a pervasive and harmful misconception that men never have to confront beauty standards or body issues. She lusted after me and it made me believe that I was something worth being desired, yet even now all those years of sexual repression lurk in the dark corners of my mind.

In the morning, we made coffee in the French press, the aroma mixing with the dew and the smoke from the fire. Abigail was bent over the hood of the Jeep smiling with her shoulders and her teeth splitting the wind. A trail led from our campsite to a pond gathered behind a crummy dam. We sat and drank our coffee on the shore where the mallards swam, twisting their heads above collared necks and giving a meek flap of their wings in quiet moments.

We went to the top of Mount Scott that afternoon. If you look far enough from the peak, you can see the fracking rigs that are lost to view when you are on the ground. I thought of all those things that were moving around me in the darkness before I lay down next to Abigail in the back of the jeep. I got sad. For a moment I felt I was part of something wild listening to the coyotes howling outside our tent as we made love. I looked then and realized there were wells among the expanse and felt deceived. Still, Oklahoma didn't look so flat from the top of Mount Scott, and it was easy to imagine we were somewhere else.

Leaning against a big rock, I asked Abigail if she'd go to Europe with me. She said she wouldn't.

"That's your future. I don't want it to turn into mine."

She never sacrificed her own vision for someone else's. I respected it. It was part of what made her so enthralling, but it hurt. In the coming months, I went out of my way to sabotage the whole thing like I tend to do, because I'm too cowardly to just end things. I'd sooner turn them toxic and make the nicer person do the hard work.

Until then, I believed we would leave the plains together. She asked if I had any interest in New York City. I'd been there once, but that was all the interest I had.

"My Aunt Joyce and Uncle Tommy live in New York. They have their hands full with their kids. I know they could use some help. They've said so. Could go up there and see what happens... You never know. You might like it. Lots of opportunities for writers in the city."

"There are too many writers in New York City."

She was always so altruistic. My desire to travel came from a pursuit of self. That was before I understood the futility of that romantic notion. We saw different futures and that drove us apart, or maybe it just wasn't built from strong things.

On the coldest night, Abigail went to pee in the woods. It was around 2 am. While she was gone, a limb fell on the tent, the poles gave out, and the mesh collapsed on top of me. I didn't fix it until morning. I made bacon and eggs in a cast iron over the fire, and Abigail pulled a tick from herself. We said goodbye to Allison and drove home in the afternoon. Before we left, we stopped and got buffalo burgers and beers at Meer's where every dish came with a side of freedom fries.

I thought about the raccoon snarling from the backseat of the jeep and it brought to mind a dumpster-dived potluck I attended with Abigail at a derelict punk house. It was an A-frame home off Lindsey street. The red and white paint was chipped all over, and you could see the gray wood that rotted underneath. On the large porch there was an old couch where everyone sat to smoke. There was a table built from scrap wood, and on top of it sat an ashtray overflowing with roaches and cigarette butts. A chandelier hung from the awning shimmering in the porch light. They hosted zine making parties, books clubs, and workshops on everything from digital security to direct action. I learned Riot Medicine 101—how to flush pepper spray from a person's eyes and use a tourniquet. There were lessons on industrial sabotage and unionizing your workplace.

A love triangle sewed several uncomfortable threads through the foundation of our activism. Every once in a while, someone wound up on the porch crying, head hanging between their legs. This particular night Terry and Mika were arguing on the side of the house. We ate ice cream that was dived from the dumpster behind Albertson's. I went to get the tub from the freezer and found a dead raccoon in a grocery sack. I opened it up to look. It was in good shape for roadkill. Its eyes were still open. The emptiness there was compounded by its lifelessness. Those beady eyes were at once soothing and inescapable. When Terry and Mika came back in, we acted as if we hadn't heard their arguing. I couldn't stop thinking about the raccoon in the freezer.

On the drive home from the wildlife refuge, we had a lot to say to one another, but we didn't talk much. It was those things that were left unsaid, the things that remained in the dark, that steered us toward the months of disarray to follow. The road was wide open and bright. I couldn't see a cloud in any direction.

A couple days later Abigail yelled at me from the shower, "God damn. It looks like a fucking tick head is still stuck in my arm pit. Will you come look at this shit?"

She was right, the head of a deer tick was lodged into the front of her armpit where her cleavage lifted from her chest.

"Can you get it out, please?"

I popped it out between my fingers and washed it down the sink. She dried off and we didn't think much about it until a few weeks later when she called me from the hospital. Abigail went home to visit her family in Tulsa. She collapsed during yoga class, and the doctor said it was stage two Lyme disease. She called and was more composed than me upon receiving the news. She said they caught it early.

"Maybe camping is just not my forté," she said.

That stubborn urge that drove us to touch one another went away. We stayed in the same house but slept in different rooms. I can't tell you if Abigail still thinks of me on certain mornings when the window is opened, glinting with dew that shimmies in the soft breeze of dawn before it makes its way through the bug screen and across the skin of her neck. It is no small task trying to untangle someone from all those unseen forces driving them to be what they are, the root of it all lying in the dark, while the jealousy and the neurosis are the only bits that show themselves. Things whirl around in the dark, and they change the way we carry ourselves, even if the cause or the shape of it all goes unseen. The body and ecocide are two sides of the same coin in that way.

I teared up when I saw that dildo shining in the windowsill. I sat for a while and watched it bend the light coming through the bamboo, thinking of coyotes and raccoons, ancient hills and rituals performed for the sun, breaking and regathering through the prism of green latex.

SOPHIE FINDS HER BODY

Sophie said her gender euphoria brought her in touch with an expansive sense of herself. I told her that I didn't know what that meant. She said it as we drove through Edmond, Oklahoma where a 140-foot cross towered over the interstate—it made her think of transmogrification which led her to consider how poorly defined our understanding of the flesh is. I could tell that she had thought about it before. Sophie had recently begun the first cycles of her hormone therapy, and small lumps were forming on her chest. She used Nair to get rid of her body hair, and she liked the ideas of Merleau-Ponty and David Abram, because they told her that all things played a role in how she built her identity. She said that's how a place could be a person and person could be a place. This realization was particularly disconcerting to her, because of something she called the Anthropocene. I learned a lot from Sophie.

We parked the car at Roman Nose and stepped out shoeless onto hot asphalt before slipping into our boots. The sun was doing funny things. It appeared to be moving quickly in a way that was inconsistent and gelatinous. The blackjacks were bright green standing out on a backdrop of red.

While walking down the trail, we listened to the elms cooing in the warmth of the wind as it blew with a hushed strength, folding the tall grass over so it pointed north toward cooler climates. There were birds chirping. I could only hear them, but I searched the trees earnestly with my eyes, and almost tripped over my feet.

"My skin seems thinner, and I can feel more of the world around me. My sense of self is tied to my body in that way too, I guess. I'm more sensitive to changes in the temperature and the wind—it's almost like it's blowing right through me."

Sophie's words were accompanied by rolling motions with her hand, as if she was hinting at interconnection with her movements.

"Whatever it is that drives that separation of me from everything around me is more delicate. I am seeing and feeling things I pushed out before... the barrier between me and the wind or me and the water isn't there. Then I wonder if it ever was, and I just needed to go through these changes to feel that. It started with the realization that gender is bogus, but from there I extrapolated, you know?"

There was a fluidity to the way she moved on the trail and it gave credence to the idea that she'd come into herself as a sort of planetary appendage. Sophie picked something from her arm and tossed it away into the grass, scratching the spot where it had been.

"Trying to be a boy never felt natural. Seems to me that things are always in a state of flux. Like the clown fish. Only the toughest, baddest males in a group get to become female. That's how I feel. So, what does that say about you?"

Sophie nudged my shoulder.

"I guess I'm not the toughest, baddest clown fish."

"Guess not."

She worked her way down into a small ravine toward a stream running between the ash trees, grasping roots that rose from the red dirt, weaving themselves into dynamic patterns and feeding on the moving water. The stream came from a spring, appearing through a big hole in the red clay, likely flowing from the Ogallala aquifer, giving me a glimpse of a hidden body that is running dry. It has been a century since the aquifer was tapped to mend the land from the ravages of the Dust Bowl. The ecological impacts of industrial farming continue, but the damage is carried out below our feet, far from sight. This is often how consent to ecocide is manufactured. Sophie became still and alert, hearing something that sounded like a rattlesnake, but then there was silence. A warmth was rising from the red dirt. Everything was dusty. It was kicked up by the wind, filling the space around my knees. The dirt hit my calves and it stung. Sophie's words were lost to the frantic movement of things.

The land around us once belonged to Henry Roman Nose, chief of the Southern Cheyenne. The tribe set up winter camp in the canyon running through the State Park, outmaneuvering Custer while raiding white settlements. Roman Nose died in the canyon. I don't know how it happened, but the gypsum cliffs look like blood. The whole state looks like it's built on mounds of dried scabs from old, untreated wounds.

"I'm not saying that everyone will feel the same things once they transition, but it's how I feel. I feel more...sensitive, more far-reaching. I am closer now to the things that I thought I only held inside my head. I felt really alone with myself. Instead, I'm beginning to feel the opposite, like my head is within them—the leaves of the cottonwoods, the clay, and the streams." She waded into the spring. It was red, cloudy. "Like the water around my calves right now, the skin down there has gotten smoother, softer, and I can feel it."

I watched her crossing through the flow, and I could see she was moving through the world in a different way. It was hard to tell if it was rehearsed or the inevitable outcome of her transition, but it felt like there was an ease to it that I couldn't see before, as she stepped through the shallow water. A sparrow was perched on an unrealized limb. The buds stood tall. I couldn't tell the sparrows from the warblers. Even now, I exist among so many things that are unknown to me. Sophie continued to move in a way that seemed too intentional. But I trusted her. It was intentional.

94

"It hurts too. It hurts not only because it hurts and my body aches, but because I have a clear head now. I see more of the suffering that is happening outside of myself, not just my own, and the extent of that suffering is painful."

It sounded like Sophie was concerned because she felt more embedded in our ecological abuses. I wasn't sure if this resulted from her transition or the framework she applied to all of the changes. It doesn't matter, I guess. Sophie said this was the pitfall of mindfulness—you become more attuned to the reality of a suffering planet. Duhka, she called it. "All these people who claim to find inner peace through the joy of mindfulness are full of shit. A mystical insurrection, an occult militancy, that's the only sensible outcome to a belief in animism and a genuine experience of interconnection."

"I hear you. For me, I get what you are saying. It clicks. But what if people don't feel that? What if they don't feel some sacred connection?"

"You don't have to, but it helps. You can come to the same conclusions through pretty simple logic and that should compel you toward a similar response. Every scientist on the planet will tell you what an absolute fuck storm we have stirred up. They will tell you that things are changing on a scale that we cannot model. They just call it the earth system."

The wind picked up and moved through her hair. She kneeled down in the water and dipped her head in so when she stood back up, her hair didn't move in the wind anymore. Instead it stuck to her shoulders in wet strips that spit streams down the curve of her back. She looked like her own planet. Her own ecosystem covered in canyons and rivers.

"Based on the urgency of the situation and the failures of our systems of power, government and capitalism, to step up to the plate, there is only one real solution..." She looked over at the black hole where the spring was emerging, trailing off and expecting me to finish her thought for her. "It's a matter of self-defense." She shrugged.

As she stepped from the stream, the wind picked up and

goosebumps covered her legs. There was a whistling sound across the reaches of the canopy, and I lay on my back, uncomfortable on the uneven ground. Sophie rose from the stream in a silken way. The water beaded on her skin. Behind her, on the other side of the spring, the earth rose until the cascading red peaked in a gentle roll turning downward below tufts of yellow grass. She moved uphill toward the open mouth of the sky. It was too blue. I don't want a sky that I can disregard. Without warning, it should go from blue to black, so the clouds swell until there's an explosion, a microburst breaking limbs, leaving them littered across the ground. Sophie was moving upward, digging her toes in and climbing to the point where the earth disappeared into the sky. I looked the other direction outside of the tree line, and it was the sky that disappeared into the earth. It was swallowed by the ground, as if it grew tired of trying to outrun the flatness that rolls across Oklahoma, so it lifted and vanished, giving up the panorama to the plains.

She looked small as she climbed further up the hill. I felt I should follow her, as I continued to look backward at the relentless unfurling. There was a weight at the center of my chest watching the land move forward, remaining dominant under the pressure of the open sky—so blue and wide, its vastness like the ocean for us landlocked creatures. There were herons flying toward the vanishing point in a muddled pattern, but they moved their wings in unison. I don't know if they disappeared into the blue or if it was the red that took them.

Looking away from the plains, I saw Sophie and the hill lifting her up and then clouds beyond. She moved forward and disappeared over the golden crest. I felt again compelled to follow, but I remained unmoving. The wind picked up and the red dirt came with it. The plains and the sky were hard to see.

WILDLAND URBAN
INTERFACE (WOO-EEE)

There was a reassuring lifelessness to the blue color of his skin. I am unsure the shelf life of a casket or an embalmed body, though I hope for a hasty decomposition someday. I was relieved to see him so still like that. He was not looking to linger. He had moved on to the next big thing. I thought of New Orleans—the Victorian neon maze and the fog that rested inside that bubble, shapeshifting and digesting our spirit, while Merchant was frantic, driving ninety miles per hour through the myth of the American south. Or could it be the Caribbean? The bored taste of cigarettes was stuck in my mouth as I stood over him. I smoked more then.

Cockroaches ran around the flame of the stove top as it burned, softening two packs of ramen. I was deep into a space bag (5 liters of cheap wine) when the phone vibrated against my leg. On the other end, Lucille, a voice from a past life, an erratic and murky fling, demanding that I go to New Orleans with her. Not later but right then. Glancing at the clock—it was past midnight—I objected. But she was convincing, as she could sometimes be. Within the hour, I was sitting in a white Jeep Wrangler with three other guys that I didn't know too well. I had shared a partner with one of them, and it was a source of jealousy for me, because I am far more progressive socially than I am emotionally.

I hadn't seen New Orleans since that great storm left it awash, and I was uncertain what to expect from a city that had risen from the dead. Resting upon a thin veil at the confluence of perception and reality, how did the Big Easy look as it tripped the Bardo? I-35 was spread out before us, paved with hopes for freedom rising from the guilelessness of our early twenties and the American promise of long highways leading to mystic visions. We had a space bag and a cellophane wrapper full of 50 mg Adderall. These things would get us to New Orleans in ten hours flat. The spirits of the American road were behind us, the ghosts of Jack Kerouac and Neal Cassady pushing us toward our final cosmic form as geeked-up Bodhisattvas. Give it a year and one of us would be dead.

We left Oklahoma with a lingering twilight rested on its back; the grasslands a mattress over which the sky stretched and night snored into the state's dry Midwestern darkness. That darkness whispered through our hair as we were stopped and standing in the sterile light of a Love's 24-hour gas station. Everything felt cold at that moment though the wind was calm and the night was warm.

I look out into the world from the belly of America, but I do not know what America is. I'm not sure if America ever really existed or if it is something that will come to be, but I know the taste of pharmaceuticals when I choke them down. When they drip. I know them like a condor knows the taste of lead. You can follow those pills down the toilet. They don't go away. They live in the sewers, polluting the groundwater, touching fish and amphibians in a bizarre ecological outcome to our isolation and discontent. Our planet is tarnished, collapsing, so we emerge from it as humans with minds that suffer, and in our pursuit of some momentary relief, we turn to prescriptions—benzos, stimulants, opiates, and opioids— that will alleviate that dizzying, fractured melancholia, if only for a bit, but they pass through our bodies and further taint the ecosystems that mingle with our senses and give us life. There exists an infinite, self-sustaining system of psychic and ecological decay caused by capitalist consumption and glimpsed in the relation of human to pill to ecosystem. Oklahoma became the first state to win a lawsuit against Johnson and Johnson for facilitating the opioid crisis, all those heavy eyes and confounded circulatory systems nodding off across the southern plains were going to get what was owed to them. I tasted the Adderall then, bitter and metallic, and I washed it down with sweet red wine.

Lucille was squeezed in next to me, and I had nothing left for her but lust. I couldn't help that, though I should have chosen not to act on it. Lucy was a painter, Polish and Kiowa, whose hands were guided by wild things, as if the ash trees and sunsets were drawing themselves when she brushed landscapes across empty space, but she also built vast and damaged worlds on canvases that leaned against the walls of her studio apartment in various stages of completion. She always wore the same set of overalls covered in iron-on patches and splattered paint. She wanted to see Buddhist monasteries among the jagged peaks of Nepal and perishing glaciers that cracked and moaned, but the opportunity to leave Oklahoma never came. Yet, her paintings vividly captured the eternal complexity of far-away places she only visited in dreams and Google searches.

On the other side of Lucille was Jerry, a heroin addict who fell victim to the American drug mythos after reading *Naked Lunch* and listening to *White Light/White Heat*. Jerry was a sharp musician and well-read. He wore black and looked sickly, but he was perceptive and sensed things from a world beyond. Practicing different stripes of southern folk magic, he was keen on hexes and built scrying mirrors from old picture frames he picked up at thrift stores. Jerry did tarot readings with a beat-up deck of playing cards and I could smell the Hoyt's cologne he wore for luck. His black pants clung to his legs. His shoulders formed to the corner of the vehicle. His thin frame shifted effortlessly within the seatbelt and Adderall was spilled in his cup holder. His facial hair was short and thick, and his eyes always seemed to be searching for something in the air around him. His chin had an angle that gave his stubble an air of cynicism for reasons that are entirely geometric and that I can't quite identify. Kenneth, who was in the passenger seat, dressed a lot like Jerry—black leather jacket, black t-shirt, black jeans that were torn and faded—but Kenneth was more attractive. He was less sickly. Despite this, Kenneth had a buck-toothed 16-year-old girl-friend he picked up after weekdays at the high school. He told the teachers he was her uncle while Sonic Youth poured from the blown speakers of his flat black truck. He record-ed music on a reel-to-reel in a room that was swarmed with bedbugs and smelled of smoke from cigarettes that he didn't smoke. Kenneth believed that the ideas for popular sci-fi movies were generated by US intelligence agencies in order to misguide the public on clandestine operations related to extraterrestrial life, time travel, and psychic warfare. Mer-chant was slumped behind the steering wheel fiddling with the locking mechanism of the hard top. Merchant wanted to know what everything meant in a way that commanded some reverence. In this world, two types of people captivate me: those that immerse themselves in figuring it all out, and those who have no interest in asking those questions.

Merchant was haunted by an existential inquisition that he exorcized with benzos and bourbon. One night he went to bed and the silence surrounding his questions consumed him. For Merchant, this was a trip into the swollen heart of white American boys who have the luxury to worry themselves sick in pursuit of arcane answers. Merchant held adventure in his eyes, looking toward a long journey that never began. He held tight to sacred ambitions, but they were clouded by an irking feeling of surrender. The driver's seat pulled at his core. The movement of the highway was coming from somewhere with-in, and he acted as an extension of the vehicle. The road was unfurling and spinning toward a destination that couldn't be understood. Everything we saw disappeared only to rise in a reflection of itself, again crumbling away, the moments gone to time. And time we cannot control.

We stopped for gas in Dallas where the skyline glistened, sketching a neon horizon, blocky and distinct in front of my eyes which strayed southward with Oklahoma and the Red River flowing behind us. We left the wind, and the night was still warm. I could see the window where Lee Harvey Oswald fired a few shots, leaving bits and pieces of young President Kennedy all over Dealey Plaza. There was a pigeon on the ground hobbling toward the scraps from some road tripper or truck driver, and it looked anchored to the concrete despite its wings.

We left Dallas heading east on I-20, and somewhere around Shreveport Merchant said, "Mind if we get off at the next exit? My grandparents' old house is only a few miles away. I spent a lot of time there before they died. I'd like to see it again if I could. Curious to know what kind of condition it's in."

We parked in front of an old green house with white accents. All the paint was chipping, and towels were hung in the windows to keep the sunlight out, but the lawn was well kept. Merchant climbed out of the Jeep and walked over to a blue beech tree growing in the front yard. It was a big thing for a beech, and I watched him touch its bark, running his hands along the trunk and talking to it before he lifted himself into the lower limbs and sat grinning, totally blissed out.

"What's he thinking about?" I asked Lucille.

"I don't know. Being a kid, maybe."

Merchant grew up in an ecology of contradictions. The promise of picket fences and then internet connection decayed, and there was nothing to become. He could only fit snugly into the spectral suit of the world he was promised. Part of a generation that went to waste, he tried to prove to himself that there is nothing better than being wasted. The last time I saw him alive, his eyes were too heavy to notice much as he swayed on the edge of a curb singing indecipherably; he never noticed I was standing there in front of him.

Merchant climbed from the tree and floated back to the Jeep, seeming to hover above the gray upholstery with an embodied weightlessness. We drove a block or two and pulled off to the side of the road, grinding out 25 mg of Adderall to put next to our brain before getting back on the road, heading into the full moon over the bustle of the east. And behind us another light rose, and then a splitting sound. A police car. They must have witnessed the whole depraved scene.

"Fuck, put this shit away," said Merchant tossing the pill-filled wrapper into the back seat.

"It's not a big deal, man. I have a prescription," said Jerry.

Merchant rolled down the window for the approaching cop.

"You know why we are pulling you over?"

"No officer."

"What was your business at that house back there?"

"That's my grandparents' house. 'Least it was before they passed away, officer. We are on our way to New Orleans, and I thought I'd stop to take a look. I'm not in this neck of the woods much anymore."

"That's a trap house now, son. You know what a trap house is?"

"Yes, sir. I've heard the term. Real sad to hear my grandparents' house has been turned into a drug den, officer. Used to climb that beech tree out front, seems a lot smaller now than it did back then."

"... you been drinking? I smell alcohol."

I leaned forward from the back seat, "I was drinking last night. Quite heavily, officer. Red wine. Cheap stuff. You're probably smelling me, I'm ashamed to say."

"You were drinking in the vehicle?"

"... No sir. I was drinking before I entered the vehicle... and sometimes at rest stops."

The cop squinted with disapproval, though his own nose was big and red and veiny from whiskey.

"Alright, y'all leave this neighborhood, and I don't want to see any of you around here again. Or I'll assume the worst."

"Thanks, sir. I don't believe any of us have a reason to come back," Merchant assured him.

The backseat of the car became uncomfortable. We stopped to refill the tank, and I stretched my legs at a Circle K that sold Slap Your Mama hot sauce and had a glory hole drilled through the yellowed porcelain on the bathroom wall. "Tuesdays 7-10 pm," scribbled above it in black marker. When I came out the sunrise had turned to morning and there was a harsh, waving quality to it that daylight takes on after nights with no sleep, and my legs felt long like they were not my own—too soft against the oil-stained concrete—and rising from the south was the wet tangle of the Louisiana swamps. I could smell them, breathing a sort of stuffy mischievousness that set itself in my mind, filling the tunnels between my thoughts like a displaced fog, followed by the sweet, sharp smell of gasoline, and they mingled, and I moved forward with them.

I sensed that we were approaching the ecosphere of New Orleans. It felt peculiar, like the final gasps of pleasure from someone dying of autoerotic asphyxiation. The roof was vibrating and everyone was battling their fatigue with the last bits of Adderall dripping down their throats. There was a *thump thump thump* as the tires beat against I-10 east of Lafayette and the swamp formed all around us, inscribing its mythology into the atmosphere with the faint smell of gasoline still stuck to the seats—that final stretch of highway was short and hazy, so we allowed ourselves to become bored with this quest for nothing in particular. Inside New Orleans, the sun and its heat were still wobbly as if rising and filling a fragile bubble, and the fog remained there with me, rising from the swamps, trapped around us, and filling my head. We left the car at a Valvoline for the day to have the oil changed.

Within moments, I was taken with a familiar yet alien certainty that New Orleans was reborn, rising from the floodwaters of Katrina and caught between planes of being and non-being. I felt it all whirling around me in conflict, but there were also moments of balance. I watched Merchant move along, and something about him reflected this. Perhaps it was how his arms hung from his shoulder or the way his head was perched on his neck. I have heard New Orleans described as both a Southern city and a Caribbean city. The cultures merged around us as we wandered the streets, blues pouring from the bodies of musicians playing only for themselves, and the hoodoo shops set up in the unlit pockets of the French Quarter.

In the last half of the 19th century, they called the place of my birth in central Oklahoma the Unassigned Lands— still Indian Territory for the most part. That was before the government came and took it for a third time. This history of colonization and Indigenous genocide remains at once ever-present and unacknowledged. The colonizers too were forced to flee when the wild reared up, and the Dust Bowl turned the western part of the state barren and desolate fifty years later. As they scattered around the country, my ancestors came to be known as Okies. It was a label that was once met with some scorn, but I don't mind it.

My grandparents were children on the plains of Oklahoma when the dry heat was being pushed around by those restless winds. They reminisce on the dustbowl from time to time. Grandad said, "My folks tried to get us out to California, but we ran out of gas in Buckeye, Arizona."

And Grandma Owens says, "I got this old cornbread mold, you know where I got it? Well, I was playing outside, you know this was during the depression, and there was this car packed, oh it makes me laugh, it was packed so high, I mean you couldn't fit another thing on there. No way. I was playing, and off came this old thing. It's cast iron you know? Real heavy, it will last forever. They went driving off, and I tried to chase them. I ran and ran, but they didn't see me, so I kept it for myself. I know everyone is wondering who is

gonna get it when I die. Well, I might just be buried with it."
I hear this story twice a year. Once on Thanksgiving and once
on Christmas.

Oklahoma remains a displaced land filled with displaced
people. Those who had their homes stolen and those who fell
on the wrong side of the wild. It offers me no sense of identity. It's not the South or the Midwest—it belongs to the Indigenous peoples that were there before us. As I've said, the land
never took kindly to my ancestors. At some point, I came to
appreciate this non-identity. It liberated me of cultural and
regional pride and became a lens through which I could view
ecocide. It is easier now to declare my loyalty to something
borderless, placeless, and abstract—something like the wild.
New Orleans gives me the impression that, like a person, a
place can be reborn, rising again from floodwaters or fracking
fluid.

Walking through the French Quarter, I noted the earth
growing from the cracks in the sidewalk; it crept through the
cobblestone to touch the sun. The wild wants nothing more
than to reclaim New Orleans, reclaim it with water and with
earth. There was a man in conversation with a doll that sat
on his lap in a stained dress. Her hair was pulled out, and
there was a dent in the side of her head above her eye. And he
said, "This is my girlfriend. She's all I have." All around him,
the wild grew into the urban sprawl and brought with it a
thinning of the veil between cityscape and the consciousness
of wildness that lies beyond, in death and in wilderness. The
people around us brought life to the streets and they reflected this interface—the crust punks and vagrants and buskers
living peripheral to the confines of capital. As we drifted
through the city, our feet were too accustomed to the flatness
of Oklahoma, and they kept getting caught on the cracks of
the sidewalks.

I bought pot from a gangly man who insisted we go
around the corner before I handed him the money. He said
his boy was around, and he didn't approve of his side business.

"He's gonna be a professional linebacker one day. Play for the Saints, I bet," he said. "He doesn't want me selling weed, but there's nothing wrong with it. I'm just trying to make people happy." He sold me a dub sack for fifteen bucks, and I was happy.

New Orleans smelled the same way a ghost would, and we were seeing the sun as something that held us by our feet, existing not six trillion miles away, but lighting the street in front of us. Our fealty to ambiguous ideas of space gave way to a sort of unguided pace, adrift in the orbit of wide-eyed trans queens and unhoused Juilliard graduates. We were still feeling the speed from the overnight trip, and we wanted the promised hoodoo loa to come to us, but we weren't prepared for it. Certainly, a veil was dissipating and one could sense the cycles moving through the urban ecology like the mystical loneliness of wilderness, in a cedar grove perhaps, or caught in the dust switching directions over the desert before the disappearing sun. The city was high, and we were high with it, the barrier between person and place rubbed away.

Again, I noticed the grass growing through sidewalks where roots of ancient oak and cypress split the concrete like reanimated tentacles rising from the ground, and the spirit of wildness produced a silent hum of grotesque splendor. The revelry came from the music rattling the mausoleums, and beside me was Lucille's sensitivity that I allowed myself to pull upon, unravelling her kindness, and she was a mirage to me then on the other side of her contempt, reborn in that moment, leaving me without any sense of who she was any-more. Time just changes things.

With a pocket full of weed and some cheap red wine, I entered an Arby's with stained glass ceilings and went to the bathroom to relieve myself. At the stall next to me was a man with hair that was caught-up and matted, tangled like vines, and he carried a backpack that looked like a turtle shell over his thin, hunched spine, crooked as it was over the urinal.

"Got weed?" he asked, and this caught me off guard, because we weren't previously engaged in conversation. I wondered if the smell was permeating from my corduroys.

"I've got a little. I can't spare any, but you are welcome to join us for a blunt."

"Not to worry, friend. I've got plenty. I can match if you want. I have a spot."

"Sure."

The shadow of Christ was spread across the granite cathedral in front of us while we got stoned and drank wine straight from the bottle, talking string theory and the inevitable contraction of the ever-expanding universe. I found the shadowed outline of the crucifixion to be comforting in that moment. Why? There was a garden and a graveyard below Christ's outstretched form, densely vegetated with weeds rising around the mausoleums. The trees were also lit up by lights that cast their shadows across the mausoleums, though they were dwarfed by that of Christ.

And the tragedy of New Orleans rested with me then, though it was overcast with the jubilance of the culture and those ideas that could only arise when we look into the face of desperation and the certainty of our abandonment. I felt on that park bench the joy persisting like silence below those things. And I looked up again at the shadow of Christ against the granite, arms that embraced the garden and the graveyard and the excess and I thought about the failure. I thought, "Yeah, this is ok."

The man hid his matted hair under a hat and said that his name was Paul. Paul recently became homeless after his third wife accused him of sleeping with her daughter. He said it was a false accusation, but of course, after she left him, he went on to sleep with her daughter. He felt no remorse about it because they never lived together and they were really just acquaintances.

Paul rummaged through his backpack for a couple minutes before pulling out a camera and flipping through photos of everyone he met over the past few months roaming the streets of New Orleans. He said there was nothing inherently spiritual about the vagabond life. And then asked if he could take a photo with us.

As we parted ways, Paul offered to take us to a colony where he slept. He said it should be fine but also it might be dangerous for Lucille. We decided against it. We could sleep in the car if we needed to.

We took some time to sit with the Mississippi until things moved into a new dimension of arcane weightlessness. And I was happy to look at the people around me and see their madness and ecstasy mimicking my own. The water had run across the Midwest and into the Mississippi which hurls through the bayous and the American psyche with spirits rising from its rip current. We were able to see them for a moment there at the mouth, all the American ghosts being lifted from the gurgling water of a stern wheel trailing a steamboat filled with tourists, and Jerry and Kenneth played music with a woman bent over her harp as her dingy, pink dreadlocks hung in front of the strings and she plucked them and the sound rose, dancing with the river. We saw it there then— the river itself dancing. And the swamp's fog held tight to my head, so I didn't know if it was real or if I was watching the wheat quaking on the plains. It didn't matter. Held by a flood that took up our memory in 2005 where everything was contained within the standing water of a hurricane wasteland, and we as citizens of the world knew it and the hurricane became us and it became our failures. A history of racial injustice rolls through this country like the vast networks of watersheds; the Arkansas River that feeds the Mississippi in front of me flows through Tulsa, Oklahoma too. In 1921 the Tulsa race massacre devastated the Greenwood district, so-called Black Wall Street, and in the structures that were rebuilt there are ghosts in the bricks. New Orleans too has haunted architecture. Just as we felt we were on the barrier of this place and some great beyond, at the whims of the hidden wilderness reemerging around us, the waters that had long known the meandering, turning rivers would soon find themselves as part of a large Gulf, which was part of a larger ocean.

Merchant's mom called in a panic, looking to recover her son from whatever hole he had disappeared into this time. I looked at Merchant. He looked happy, and he told his mom that he was happy. You could hear her voice, rushed and tumbling over itself through the phone. He kept reassuring her that he was safe, and she insisted on getting him a room at the Days Inn in Baton Rouge, and that is where we slept for the night.

In the morning, I followed Lucille's green eyes as they worked the room over, and I felt shame for knowing that she once cared deeply for me, and that I didn't cut ties smoothly. It is a guilt that is common to me, as I've navigated my tangles with intimacy. Lucy and I crept from the hotel room to feel the warmth of morning for a while, sitting on a curb in the parking lot, and both of us knowing that this would be our last misguided hurrah together, that time had worked in the way it does to chisel down feelings and commitment.

"This is the furthest I've ever been from Oklahoma. It feels funny down here. Doesn't it? It feels different," she said.

"Yeah, I guess it does... that was a good night. I'm glad you called. For a while, I thought I'd never see you again."

"It was quite a night. You know there was a time when you really meant something to me. I mean you still mean something to me, but for a while it felt special. Then you disappeared and I got over it, and now here you are, and I feel close to you but more like a brother again."

She leaned her head on my shoulder.

"We were friends, and then things went the way they did and wires got crossed or something and we didn't know what was what with all those feelings spinning around each other. We're still young. I don't expect us to know what we are doing...Anyway, you're a real prick sometimes and I can be needy and I am glad it's over, but these last couple days together have been nice... and it feels good to bookend this with something that feels right."

She took a deep breath through her nose and looked up at the sky to see that it was clear and blue and wet and carrying the weight of the rays of light millions of miles long traveling past Mercury and Venus to heat the asphalt at the Days Inn in Baton Rouge, the smell of the wetlands clinging to it all in a fog that shrunk and held together our sincerity and then it drifted away and my mind felt empty again as did the day.

"It's awfully muggy here. I'm gonna go get a pastry, maybe guzzle down some of that watery black shit they're calling coffee," said Lucille.

"Alright, I'll see you inside."

I looked over the parking lot toward the road and watched a Mercury drive by and then a Saturn, and I lay back against the sidewalk where my t-shirt picked up the dead leaves of a shrub planted outside of the motel. I shook them off and they floated to the ground and I left them there.

Back in Oklahoma, the familiarity reinforced a returned sense of reality as the wind picked up. A habitual silence exists below the wind, waiting for a stillness to come again, and when the silence joins that stillness they dance without motion. I hear the chatter of autumn's dying leaves as our voices quiet, and within all those empty promises and outstretched apologies that paved our road there was some peace. I took a moment to register the decay that came with the days, my skin agitated and showing some cuts, and I felt a hunger that skipped stones across an otherwise placid mind. I was letting myself cling to the noise, though the silence was ever-present.

I returned to New Orleans some years later, and the fog set in my mind so thick that I couldn't feel much. It was like an over-spiced, exotic dish that set too firmly in my taste buds, so that it overtook all the flavor that it once accentuated. And I knew that it wasn't the town, that it was me. I was in another failing relationship, and I knew that it wasn't the woman, that it was me.

And still, the weeds and the roots broke through the sidewalks, growing between the bricks on the traveled streets, and I myself had traveled more but was unable to refine my experiences in hope of rendering something that could be considered growth. The days moved quickly still, and I have nothing to say about that trip, though I longed for it to be something else so that I could again experience the ghosts rising from the Mississippi and the closure that came and laid itself before me so that there was nothing left but certainty.

Merchant died sometime before dawn when the morning was taking its time, sleeping in a bedroom in his sister's home. He went to Alaska still searching for himself. I'm sure that someone told him that that's a good place to rediscover your soul through wilderness, but sometimes you just see something beautiful and then you die.

The funeral was held in a megachurch inside a failing mall on the outskirts of Oklahoma City. The regional preacher led the service over a stream from his office in Houston, speaking to Merchant's unwavering faith in God and Jesus and all that. Kenneth and Jerry played a song on stage, Blackbird by the Beatles, if my memory serves me. They put a picture of Merchant up on the projector. He was in a bush plane outside of Juno, and he had a nice smile.

THERE IS A SINKHOLE IN WINK, TEXAS (AND IN ME)

If you follow the plains across southwest Oklahoma, you'll have the misfortune of finding yourself in Texas. You keep going long enough and you'll run into a town called Wink. In Wink, you'll find a big hole. As a matter of fact, you'll find two big holes. I may have said it before, but the plains stretch too far to be poked on much. The ground starts moving in ways it shouldn't, and before too long you're going to have yourself a sinkhole or two. And then there remain four-thousand miles of beat up geology surrounding those sinkholes, all of it at risk of caving in and consuming everything that rests on the surface.

As people reflect the place they came to be, all the flaws pierce through their character and their faces become marred by the holes in the hills, in the plains, in the skies, but the holes aren't carried only by the face, they open up inside, and, like those punctures in the land, something dark starts leaking out. When your spirit is thin, pulled like Oklahoma in every direction, it doesn't take much to let the darkness loose. We've been swimming in it all our lives, damming a river with a dish cloth. At some point we let go, and it takes us away.

I was sunk into the ground beside Isaac, resting in the shadow of an old rig that bobbed and creaked south of Kitchen Lake. Having recently returned from two years wandering the Balkans and Eastern Europe, I was already itching to leave. I wanted to see Montana, mountains still aging to maturity and rivers rushing, snarling undammed down the slopes of the continental divide.

The wheatgrass rose around us, languid and swaying with all the time in the world. The rig's ceaseless mechanical moan was a metronome that jostled memories of Grandpa Bryson's third wife, Martha. She chiseled into my young mind images of children dismembered while scaling the chugging parts of old giants much like this one. It's technology of a bygone era, an aging appendage of industry before the fracking boom transformed the state and the process of oil extraction. I remember the old public service announcements from daytime TV warning kids not to climb on the rigs. Looking back, it seems odd because the oil industry went on to take our bodies from us anyway. Reilly Thompson was twenty-two when he fell from a fracking rig after a gasket blew, dropping thirty feet. He'll walk with a cane for the rest of his life. They reassigned him to the security office, where his nights are spent in front of the cameras, nursing the chronic pain that surges through his thigh.

Isaac tapped my shoulder and handed me what could barely pass for a joint. The sky was a blank slate of pale blue. The sun burned through the last stand of wheat grass that grew tall and cracked. I hopped to my feet and dusted off my clothes, leaning over the chain link fence that enclosed the old rig.

"We should go for a walk," I said.

"Sure."

Sutton Trail runs for a mile and a half around a large pond in what is called an urban wilderness park. Along the shore, we hopped from boulder to boulder. The sun was setting, casting a shadow across the pond that bled through the dusk. Somewhere, ravens in conversation. Their croaks and caws almost sounded intelligible. I'm certain that long-ago, when we still listened, we could decipher their meaning. I stuffed my shoes into my backpack and walked through the shallow water along the shoreline. The last leaves of autumn rode time in slow motion down, down toward the pond's murky waters.

"You think you will be happy up there?" Isaac asked.

"Where?" I replied.

"Montana. You think you'll find some peace?"

"Peace... I don't know. Mountains, at least. Wild rivers."

"Yeah, I hear it's pretty. You get used to that shit, though. Eventually it will fade into the background. You need people, community. You got that here," he said.

"Yeah, I've got that, I guess, but this place is too flat. It's like it's endless in every direction," I said.

The algae and mud squeezed through my toes and tadpoles swam in frantic circles around my ankles.

"It gives me anxiety, all that emptiness. Seems like it goes on forever unbroken except by the tower downtown and the oil rigs. You know how they call that area over near the panhandle Llano Estacado? It's Spanish for Staked Plains. Travelers had to put markers down, otherwise they'd walk a hundred miles in one direction and end up in the same place they started. It's too flat here. Too open. Plus, I've got to get out of this relationship. We hate each other, and neither of us have any place to go but home every day," I said.

"I've never had any desire to leave Oklahoma," he said. "It's always felt right. You know I was raised a Jehovah's Witness. I met the mother of my first two kids through the church. They take the Jesus shit pretty serious. I told them I was beginning to question my faith and they dropped me fucking quick."

There was a small splash in the pond. A ripple lingered. Isaac stared into the water. He looked for some sign of what had been there.

"They dropped me quick. I mean you know the story. It was friends who carried me after that, particularly friends with amphetamines. And it wasn't just my family I'd lost. I lost God then, and everything that came with that. Purpose, morals, answers, an afterlife. You lose certainty in those things and you've got to find a new way to sketch out your existence. The drugs would do it, you know, draw everything out for a little while. I had myself a blueprint of the cosmos done in disappearing ink. But when the high recedes and all those structures just...vanish...you feel more lost than before. Nevertheless, you keep doing it for those moments of certainty, willing to have it all come crashing down again and again."

Isaac stood up, his long legs extending with a stiff pop. He approached a tree and locked eyes with a fungus that stuck out from the bark. He touched it.

"I think that's called alders bracket," I said.

"It's been a while since I've gone back to the drugs. You know that, though. Third kid straightened me out pretty good. Guess I let him give me that purpose, answer all those questions about the universe and life and all that shit. Not saying I'm right in doing it, just saying caring for a child has got to be a better purpose than cradling that nasty pipe."

I took Isaac's moment of vulnerability and made it about myself. I was leaving Oklahoma because I wanted to flee my own desolation. Like Isaac, I felt there was a hole inside me. And perhaps I was wrong, place and land and wildness might not bring me solace. And even then, if God was something I was supposed to see everywhere, why was I so unnerved by the expanse of the plains?

A mile into the trail we ventured through the woods and found a tarp strung up between two crooked trees. Inside was a heap of beat up old sleeping bags and piss-stained blankets strewn with various bottles of cheap vodka and malt liquor. Twigs snapped below our feet and something wrestled from the pile. We jumped away, startled. A possum froze and flipped on its back. Its lips pulled from its teeth, and its anal glands started secreting a rancid odor that mimicked a rotting carcass. We left it like that.

The sun was almost gone as we approached the lot where we'd parked the car. It was still as empty as when we'd arrived.

The plastic door handle was already cold. I was afraid to go home, so I didn't.

Ambient neon pressed into the stench of cheap beer and American Spirits. An aura, time bending and vaporous red, emanated from the building where the door was propped open and the crowds gathered along the sidewalk overflowing into the street. Almost magical. The Deli is the pulse of Norman, the hub of its various subcultures. The town would lose half its character if it ever closed up. It's a gathering place for the artists and eccentrics—the people who make Norman a haven of creativity among the sweep of capitalist decadence. Rowdy music was cutting and spinning just above the drunken chatter. Everyone was zoned in, sorting out who they were going home with for the night. A little empty lust just to kidnap time. Everything was caught in that tangled web of flirtation, and I was on my fifth beer. It was all I could do.

Doka Dawg stood outside taking short, hasty drags from his cigarette. You could call Doka Dawg a hippie hustler. He's an Osage with a slick, black ponytail running along the ridge of his spine like a great stallion. He stood outside the Deli with one hand in the pocket of his jean shorts, nodding his head and sniffing occasionally. Doka is a lot of man. He takes up some space. He ordered lotion in bulk from China and rebottled it in little containers that said things like *Spirit of the Wolf* and *Native Knowledge*, then resold them for 15 dollars a pop to white kids in drug rugs.

Standing beside Doka Dawg, there was an older man in a Grateful Dead tie-dye with a head full of thinning dreads who everyone knew as Star Dog. Star Dog curates Norman's music scene. He hosts big parties on a plot of land at the edge of town. If you're invited to play one of those gigs, you've touched the echelon of local stardom. He plays lyrically pornographic folk music that brings to mind old Wavy Gravy songs, and he's shared a stage with David Allen Coe and the Flying Burrito Brothers.

The music poured onto the streets from the inside, nimble and inspired that night. I saw Margo. I was swaying a bit. Margo lost her two front teeth in a bicycle accident that happened years ago. Five dots are tattooed under each of her eyes, and the phases of the moon are spread across her chest.

"Hey Margo, how's it going?"

"Door man won't let me in."

"Why not?"

"Because he's an asshole." She looked over her shoulder at the door man and raised her voice. "Yeah, I'm talking about you... asshole!"

"Really Margo, I'm the asshole? You took the tip jar and face planted before you made it out the door! Shit, you can't come back for at least a month. Why don't you take this time to dry out a little bit, huh?"

"Prick..." Margo muttered under her breath.

I left the Deli and walked through the streets, along bricked alleys marked with graffiti, feeling the dull throb of music from clubs and cars. The streetlights cast a milky orange haze across the cracked concrete and crumbled red brick, climbing to the rooftops and electric poles. There was a bicycle tied to a lamp post and behind it two people embraced, kissing deeply against the wall, half-hidden in the shadows.

The old local businesses were being run out one by one. I looked at the "For Rent" sign in what used to be a head shop that was raided by Norman PD. The cops were becoming increasingly militarized. I witnessed the beginning of it during my years in town. More body armor and a growing number of assault rifles. The cops suggested a quarter million dollars of taxpayer money be spent on the acquisition of a BearCat—a tank equipped with gun ports, battering rams, and methods for delivering tear gas. It is the same all across America, and the brutes are unrepentant. Some might call the bloodthirst a toxic culture, but I consider it a dark psychic network of minds untethered from souls.

Looking up, I saw the stars only as specks faded through the cover of the town's light. Approaching Lion's Park, a troupe of fire dancers were spinning flames that melted into a single sinuous pattern morphing from circles to Xs to pulsing, fluid signs of infinity. The dancers were in a deep focus, a flow state, *wu wei* as the Taoists call it. No mind. A meditative, primal connection to the element of fire radiated from their movements, exhibiting its beauty and a reverence for its destructive capacity as they weaved and contorted their bodies to avoid coming in contact with it. The flames were captured in countless reflections in the sweat beading on their skin. I sat and watched for half an hour before I walked home.

I fell into my bed feeling blissful and satisfied, then the morning came and I woke up. My head felt too swollen for my skull, and I only thought of greasy food. The window unit couldn't keep up with the heat. I was sweating into my jersey sheets, jammed up in a web of grim mindfulness.

I couldn't handle the plains any more. It was a good idea to move. I was sure of it. The sticky heat swept across the mid-American stretch and picked up everything, so that hole revealed itself inside of me. I'd come of age on the buckle of America's deteriorating Bible Belt, cinched tightly around the necks of pregnant cheerleaders and emaciated opioid addicts. Over this flat place we were suspended in disbelief, undulating above pools of oil, swimming with the piranhas of the plains.

I often felt like shit. When I did, I stared at far away things, cypresses and stars, reveling in the splendor of knowing that those distant objects were part of my perception, and I felt better, as if the world was at all times sending itself to dance with my senses. But those meditations were becoming less reliable.

That desolation, the big empty hole that Isaac was talking about, I held it too. I hopped in and out of that void hoping to find something to cushion my fall. Instead, I continued to mine myself for scarce resources, looking for a quick fix to a problem that could mar my life if I didn't figure out why it was so keen on haunting me.

I looked into the mirror, and I saw my Grandpa Bryson—round nose and thin hair fixed onto the ghost of myself. A hundred different pieces held together by the darkness that flows underneath the plains. Deep inhalations to fill a balloon ruptured by legions of pinholes, lightheaded and out of breath.

Devon Tower rises from downtown Oklahoma City, sending a stern message to the people of Oklahoma: your future is in the hands of the oil industry. It rises and pokes a hole in the sky, right beside those holes in the atmosphere. Through that hole, a bright light comes shining through. You'd think that someone opened a window to heaven if you didn't know it was the sun reflecting off the veneers in the conference room on the 50th floor.

Likewise, there were holes in me that needed to be reckoned with. They never seemed to fill up no matter how much beer and whiskey I poured down them. When I spread out in the Oklahoma grass, feeling the trembling earth beneath me, I got pulled in every direction and those holes got bigger.

After the fracking boom, Oklahoma went from three earthquakes a year to two earthquakes a day. Dormant faults shook to life. They keep doing what they're doing and Oklahoma will be a sinkhole too, piercing through the plains. That sweet-smelling golden wheat that once blew in the wind, now blown away, where the plains stretched, strained and sweating at the foothills of elder mountains. A stronghold to those barons in the sky looking down, gazing into the sinkholes of a future they've manufactured. It'll be America's very own God-hole right through the belly of this country.

KENT COOPER FONDLES
THE ARISTOCRACY

Kent Cooper is a dealer of catline booms, hoist lines, drilling lines, monkey boards, traveling blocks, top drives, masts, drill pipes and doghouses. All the parts that keep the oil rigs of the Great Plains a-chuggin'. When Kent Cooper looks to seduce the out-of-state sleaze that fly in to sort through the logistics of their plundering, first he orders a stretch limousine. Not just any stretch limousine, but a pearl white twenty-passenger Cadillac Escalade named Angel. It's a thing to behold. Celestial. Kent Cooper gets these bigwigs a suite down at the Skirvin, a newly renovated hotel smack dab in the middle of Oklahoma City. It is only a few blocks away from the Devon Energy building, extending from the Oklahoma City skyline, a phallic eyesore, short on subtlety, but a neighbor to the heavens, seating the CEOs damn near divinity just the way they like it.

I know this because, in the recent past, when Kent Cooper wanted Angel, he called me. I picked up his potential clientele in that heavenly extended sedan and drove them three blocks to Oklahoma's premier restaurant, the Mantle, serving the upper crust since 1994. Kent Cooper is morbidly obese and the restaurant's small portions of artisanal cuisine never quite hit the spot, so we regularly finished the night at iHop, drowning plates of pancakes in maple syrup with extra sides of bacon.

After dinner at the Mantle, I drove them to the Trophy Room, a gentleman's club off interstate 240, a two-story palace of debauchery in south Oklahoma City, the so-called Mexican part of town, gang territory belonging to the Southside Locos. A fine place for rich white men to get dirty while eluding the gaze of their bourgeois brethren.

As we drifted through town inside Angel, that hallowed chariot of decadence, they talked of the cocaine and thirteen-year-old prostitutes in Guatemala. A place they'd fly their private jets on a whim for a weekend of hedonism on the company card.

After a few hours inside the Trophy Room, they stumbled out with dancers on their arms paid to accompany them back to their hotel room. One evening we returned to the Skirvin, where I opened the limo door and the ladies started filing out. One of them looked at me and said, "Woah, dude, what's up? It's me, Jenna. From high school. Remember me?"

"Oh yeah... what's up Jenna? How you been?"

"Pretty good. Makin' money. I'm pullin' in like five G's tonight, and this dude is taking me to Dallas tomorrow for a new set of tits. I can't complain. Man, I miss the old days, though. Miss those high school parties we used to have. We were so crazy! Are these guys paying you alright?"

"Not that great, apparently."

She turned to the swaying troupe of lusty barons. "Y'all, I know this dude. You better take care of him, 'cause we go way back."

I gave them a nervous smile and raised my eyebrows.

They staggered forward pulling out their wallets, "Of course, baby, of course." They started passing me 100-dollar bills. One of them turned toward me and added, "Can you go pick up some condoms, though?"

I returned to the Trophy Room to find Kent Cooper. He insisted that I get a dance from three women at once. After a brief expression of reluctance, I agreed to it, because I knew that Kent Cooper wouldn't accept an outright dismissal of his offer. It would be taken personally, and it would cut into my tip at the end of the night. What can I say? I was a product of my environment.

Kent Cooper had a wife and kids that he left for weeks at a time. While we were together, he got phone calls from his children asking where he was. He said that he needed time to himself. That he would come back home when he got his head cleared. He kept his thin mistress at the Holiday Inn two blocks from the Trophy Room.

TRANSMOGRIFIED

Our church practiced communion in the form of the Eucharist. The hall of worship echoed and shook with the guilt of real estate agents and booze-soaked general contractors. It felt like the whole damn place could come crashing down like Sodom and Gomorrah under the weight of all that guilt. The grape juice was sweet. The crackers were bland. Flesh and blood to re-assimilate the presence of Christ into our lost little souls courtesy of Sam's Club. I never really understood the concept of transmogrification, but I wanted to keep that divinity burning inside me, so I snacked and I slurped and I hoped that did the trick.

The preacher who blessed the wine and crackers got into some trouble for shooting his neighbor's dog. It wasn't in cold blood. The mutt kept killing his chickens, so he got fed up and shot him. I remember the preacher's big red mustache, and the way he talked over my head like I wasn't there. I guess he suspected he couldn't fish a tithe from the shallow pockets of a nine-year-old boy.

We walked into the sanctuary through the heavy doors on Sunday mornings when the sky was blue and puffy, bloated with heat and sunlight. The service began with music, the dimmed lights glowed from the stage and sent a shadow arching behind a thin man banging wildly on his tambourine, mad with the lord's inspiration. A single tuft of hair stuck from his balding head, waving back and forth with his crazed gyrations.

At the end of each sermon and before communion, the preacher performed baptisms. There was a pool on the back of the stage that rippled and sparkled throughout his sermon. *The wages of sin can only be washed away through acceptance of the savior.* He waded in wearing long red robes and the soon-to-be-reborn followed in white. They stood in the water as sinners but came out as servants. I wondered what they were in-between, as they were submerged—a Schrodinger's cat of divine redemption. What goes through the mind of someone under water during the moment of baptism? Are they filled with anxiety, mulling over the fact that they'll emerge from the waters with an obligation to the rigid morality of a demanding God, or are they just hoping the water doesn't get in their nose on the way up? I guess everyone is a different sort of Christian.

I remember diving in the warm waters of the Caribbean where it was so clear I could see for a hundred yards, like looking out on the plains in autumn when the heat wasn't burning through and singeing the clarity of things. Except there were seahorses and eels, and all the sounds were throbbing and intensified like I was listening to a trombone filled with jelly while the seaweed moved with it all in a flowing dexterity.

When I dove I paid close attention to my breath. I made sure to breathe slowly, so I didn't waste oxygen. Don't waste oxygen. All my hair stood up in the salt water. Once, a green sea turtle soared beside me and looked at me side-eyed, aware that I didn't belong, sensing I was out of my element. The turtle drifted through the water barrel-chested, flippers spread out as if it had done a belly flop and was floating in a state of empty-minded bliss.

I grabbed a handful of sand. It drifted through me like I was a ghost. Something half there. The sand settled back onto the floor of the ocean. It would never be the same, misplaced by my thoughtless fingers.

My folks never had me baptized. They said it was a choice

that I should make on my own, and by the time I was old enough to make it, my faith had fallen to the wayside. I got saved a couple times when I felt I was in need of it, but I never took the plunge, so to speak.

After my faith waned, an irking void revealed itself. All those answers and certainty disappeared, collapsing in on one another, and the structures that held up my understanding of the world around me went away, giving no warning of their impending betrayal. Like all the angels turned out to be police informants that'd been having a party in my cerebellum since I was able to think. Initially there was a sense of loss rather than liberation. There was no more Sam's Club communion, no holy exchange, and that left me pretty lost but still looking for something to chew and swallow that made me feel godly.

It was one of those weird summer nights when the grass underneath me was humming in a deep, melting voice like it was singing R&B. I lay there wide-eyed, mouth agape somewhere in the Czech countryside outside of Kutna Hora, home of the Sedlec Ossuary where chandeliers and furniture were built from the bones of peasants and soldiers killed in the Black Plague and Hussite Wars. I left Prague by train to escape the lights and watch the Perseid meteor shower. It was cloudy that afternoon, and I was concerned that the shower might be hidden behind an overcast sky, but I needed to get out of town. Prague can be a heavy place because it asks so little of you.

As night came, the clouds cleared. The campfire put off a bellied glow underscoring the galactic production in the sky, the sparks lifted themselves toward twilight with the help of a soft wind. I drank in greedy, complete gulps from my bottle of Becherovka, a Czech herbal bitter that tasted like sweet ginger in a whirlwind of spices. The evening was warm and dynamic. A bouncing horizon impregnated with remnants of the sun setting and giving off a purple aura as the meteors appeared through the sky in celestial paper cuts. The matrix of night lit up in a robotic dance, moving in tune with my senses.

The next morning, while trying to hitchhike back to Prague, a field of blossoming nettle caught my eye. It was glowing in an erotic, swelling purple, pulsing in the heat of the sun. I was into its presence, its way of being. There was a self-effacing beauty to it. I ran into the field and touched its blossoms. I let it wash through me. My face began to swell, contorting and becoming discolored above my left eyebrow. Not all nettle will cover you in a set of biochemical irritants, but this was *Urtica dioica*. With my face inflamed and discolored, it blew any chance I had of hitching a ride. I looked like an inbred creep who crawled from the backwoods and maybe I was. I went to the train station and spent what little money I had to get back to Prague.

On the train ride, I watched the fields stretch out in a collage of greens and purples, rubbing shoulders as they swayed, merging with my thoughts and producing a sense of songful euphoria. Maybe the pleasure of the meteor shower at dusk left me intoxicated with all the things I was seeing that morning wandering the Czech countryside. It was a clear day and sometimes I get caught in a passing lunacy when the sun is shining. There was an overwhelming sense that I was enmeshed with the nettle and needed to be closer to it. Through a fit of eco-erotic delirium, I was compelled to embrace it.

I sat sweating, face contorted, burning and tingling, staring from the window until the train got back to Prague. I felt great. *Is this what they call mindfulness?* I could make a conscious decision to see how far my eyes, my nose, my ears, my tongue could take me—really put those neurons to work. The planet didn't owe me anything. The nettle made it clear, there are boundaries to its generosity. Following my senses completely had left me vulnerable.

You get puffed up like that, wanting to feel everything, and you'll eventually take in the bad stuff too. When I returned to Oklahoma, I was too willing to feel all the anxiety of the plains. My environmental imagination became shaped by the burden of our impact on the aquifers, the shale formations, the wolves, the monarch butterflies, the watersheds. I was witness to the constraints of my senses and a sadness in my inability to process the grief for things that were both a part of me and so much larger than myself. Climate change and mass extinction. I faced the chaos and madness of the turning tides that are leaving ecosystems awash in the uncertainty of catastrophic ecological changes.

The plains can be a mean place, and the people who stick to them tend to get hardened. The needs of others become a burden and self-preservation the primary ambition. All that Christianity doesn't seem to evoke much empathy. Your soul stretches across the land and with all that flatness it becomes thin. If too many people start pushing on it, you get afraid it's going to pop and your spirit will come leaking out into the world, so you keep everyone away except your family who end up doing most the pushing and popping anyway.

Back in Oklahoma, my time became a practice of blotting out days, counting away the seconds of my life working in a meat freezer at an organic grocery store. That was after I was promoted from custodian. I walked through the door and entered a fugue state for eight hours, only to go home to a relationship that made me wish I was still in the meat freezer. There was a large field outside of town where I lay on warm afternoons to avoid going home. The sun baked the meat juice into my clothes. I kicked over the "For Sale" sign and wandered through the grass collecting rose rocks, or some folks call them desert roses. Swirling composite crystals made of gypsum, baryte, and sand.

I was a vegetarian butcher. Fortunately, it wasn't something they asked about on the job application. I worked with a group of guys who were perpetually tired of the boss's shit, and we talked for hours about the miserable work conditions but never did anything about them. We had shitty health care plans with high deductibles that sucked up a quarter of our paycheck every week. We received a ten percent employee appreciation discount, but the store wasn't meant for working people like us.

The head meat cutter, Robert, was dedicated to the butchering profession. The words "dead" and "meat" were tattooed across his knuckles. On the same night he got that ink he convinced his ex-girlfriend to get the "USDA Prime" emblem tattooed on her ass. I think she regretted it.

I arrived at five AM to check-in and unload thousands of pounds of cow and chicken parts. This wasn't my job. It was above my paygrade, but the manager didn't feel like doing it. I emerged from the meat freezer covered in blood, guts, and juice.

I worked with an obese, thinly bearded, and fiercely conservative man named Craig who disappeared into the bathroom twice a day for forty-five minutes. He left during the busiest part of the shift, around five o'clock, as customers rolled in after work to pick up rotisserie chickens and organic soda for dinner. He wore camo pants with a pocketknife that he sharpened on the department's whetstone while making passes at the young girl who worked in the bakery. We got into a heated argument about removing Andrew Jackson's face from the twenty-dollar bill. I thought it was a bad thing to celebrate America's history of genocide. He called me an SJW, which kinda surprised me, because I've also been accused of being insensitive, even morally cretinous, depending on who you're talking to. Craig was thirty-two, single, and still lived at home with his parents. One day he left for the bathroom during the evening rush and never came back.

Once a week a middle-aged woman with thick make-up smeared across the bronzer below her purple, permed hair ordered our biggest filet mignon. She asked us to cut it into little pieces. Ten pounds of jewelry hung from her leathered skin. One evening she said, "I'm going to have to watch you cut it this time. Last week the pieces weren't small enough, and Taffy choked on it."

"Taffy?"

"Yes, Taffy." She pulled her phone from her purse and flashed a picture of a Yorkshire Terrier.

"Oh, I see. So, this filet mignon is for... Taffy... your Yorkie."

"Yes, and last week the pieces were too big and she choked, so from now on I'll have to watch you cut it."

An hour after dicing Taffy's filet mignon, a flying wedge of asiago cheese hit me in the chin. There was a gray-haired, coupon-clutching germaphobe on the far side of the meat counter. It was Susan. Susan was a minor nemesis, well known among the staff. She always gave us grief about the position of our beard nets or the sterility of our rubber gloves. Susan demanded that we put them on in a certain order to reduce the contamination of her uncooked meat. I wondered if she forgot that it still needed to be cooked. Or maybe she ate it raw in the darkness of her home, on a bed of expired coupons like some sort of grotesque, vampiric baby boomer.

"Want some flies for lunch?" she asked.

I looked down at the dead fly on the vacuum wrapped asiago. I didn't even work in dairy. The corners of her mouth were curled up in a smile of revulsion and pleasure.

After my shift, I went to the field with the rose rocks. The clouds moved past my eyes riding the heavy breaths of the plains' forgotten gods. Great wild horses moving through the sky. A stampede that sent wind gusts across that flat, desolate, broken world. It was all I could feel. The wind caught dust and moved it through the air in a haze that shook and trembled as it changed shapes, projecting itself in an image that left as the seconds drifted away from me. That was the only thing I felt. The seconds drifting away from me.

I fled Oklahoma in a haze of desperation. In part, to escape my partner. She used to beat me up and down, leave me lying with my head tucked into my stomach and hoping she didn't find an object to start wailing on me with. Eventually, she'd wear herself out. I can't blame her. She had taken her share of whoopings. After so long, a person isn't the same. You get stuck with a bad head even if you've got a good heart. And I can be a hard person to get along with. Still, I used to have thoughts of her pulling out the old .38 revolver that I kept in my closet, underneath the blue and white quilt handed down from my mother, and leaving my thinker spread across those sweat-soaked jersey sheets, her eyes upon me, pale blue like suffocated lips.

We didn't know each other that well when she moved in. She was in a rough spot and didn't have anywhere to go. She'd been floating around from one couch to another, so I let her stay with me for a while. My apartment was small, dilapidated, barely standing. In the beginning, everything seemed brighter because of the chemicals we brought out in one another. The colors of the world were more vibrant, more consuming. We filled our apartment with orchids and ivy. There was an herb garden that lined the window in the kitchen. We got a betta fish. The place almost seemed livable, but things went downhill pretty fast. Everything became dull before too long. She killed the fish when she pushed over our shelf in a fit of rage. Eventually it was like I was seeing the world through one of those nets that old ladies wear to funerals.

I'll tell you about it. I'll tell you about the night I knew I had to leave or one of us was going to die in that shithole apartment. Maybe in the clogged-up shower or on the toilet where we covered ourselves with an empty trash bag because of the leaky pipes upstairs, or maybe at the bottom of the stairwell where the wood ached and moaned every time we took a step. Either way, it wasn't going to be glamorous.

I was being fussy, being a real bastard, because she was lying to me about seeing another man, and I was jealous. She took to swinging on me as I was sitting on the couch hurling mean words. I got up and walked to the dinner table, hoping she wouldn't follow me to the kitchen. She followed me to the kitchen. We continued hollering and cursing till she ripped the wire frame glasses from my face, stomping them to pieces on the linoleum tile, then screamed as she shattered a Tibetan salt lamp, and even amid all of that commotion, it struck me as ironic.

I got up and ran. She lunged to block the door, but I got there quick enough. When I got into the driver's seat of the car, my senses returned, and I realized that I couldn't see a thing. The bits and pieces of my glasses were spread out in the darkness of that kitchen, and the rain was coming down hard.

Then I did something I shouldn't have. You know those little bullshit decisions that become pivotal? This was that. I walked through the rainfall back into the apartment, and I went into the kitchen. The light didn't work. It wasn't the bulb, but some malfunction in the wiring. Down on my hands and knees, I searched for the scattered pieces of my glasses. She came from the back room reinvigorated and started kicking me in the stomach. I felt my organs moving around in there. Then one got me square in the face. Missed my nose but busted my lip. I was happy I wasn't picking my teeth up from the cracked linoleum. Happy I was only spitting blood instead of incisors. I pushed her away hoping for a moment of reprieve. Hoping to get out of there with one lens and a piece of bent frame, but her feet got caught up in the legs of the table, and she fell back and hit her eye on the corner of the stove. My stomach sank through the floor. Felt like it was floating in the stagnant water of the empty basement. More leaky pipes. She came up with a cut bleeding over a black eye. I felt such shame.

The white caps wrapped the peaks of the Tetons penetrating the horizon, as if they cushioned the prodding discomfort of the jagged edges plunging into the gray-blue sky, now coughing snow and howling. I was on my way to Montana. There was something magnetic about the promise of that wilderness. The lawlessness of an ecology untamed by the minds and hands of humans. I've never been one for authority, and I'd always glamorized the West. When I saw the Tetons, I was debilitated, overcome with awe. I pulled over and teared up on the side of the road. It was mid-July, and the snow fell like feral cotton balls melting onto the lenses of my spare set of glasses. The pads had come off long ago and they rubbed punctures into the crown of my nose. My skin felt like it was creeping outward in a prolonged stretch. The roots of my hair tingled. I sat on the ground, back against the front bumper of my car, chin resting in my hands, and I couldn't distinguish the chill of melted snow from the tears drying on my face.

The jagged rocks bit into the blue sky, the sky that haunted me all my life, and I felt vindicated. There was a sense of communion. Something like the pastor told me I was supposed to get from juice and crackers. The nettles and the meteors and gar hinted at it. But I knew this was momentary. It wouldn't stay, because these mountains don't always heal. They are just mountains. That's magic one moment and pain another. The back of my car was loaded with everything I had. Everything I owned stuffed into a hatch-back. Mid-July and the snow was coming down. It showed no sign of letting up.

I was born into a funny time. We can no longer know the earth as it was. Once everything was gone, all the truths I held, I was able to see more clearly what was ahead. The reflection of the wilderness, within and without, doesn't have to provide answers. There is no code of morality to something tarnished, threatened, and untamed. You go around caught in observation, taking everything in, and you're going to feel the suffering there, eventually. You notice that the white caps of the Tetons aren't sticking around as long as they used to. But when the snow melts, the mountains are still here.

THE SAME OLD THINGS,
THEY ALWAYS REFUSE TO DIE

Grandma Owens was scrubbing plates in the kitchen, her hair perfectly parted and lightly blown by the southern breeze that rustled the leaves of the pecan tree and came through the open window above the sink. She was wearing her favorite set of blue jeans, faded but starched and ironed. Grandad grumbled and cursed in his recliner watching old John Wayne westerns from behind a big glass of buttermilk. A tall cedar fence lined the backyard. I was five or six.

Uncle Dale chewed Skoal. That's when things were right with the family business. Brothers were betrayed and money was lost, so he chews Grizzly now, but back then it was always Skoal. Empty cans of long-cut wintergreen littered his truck and his bedside table. He pinched a horseshoe between the index finger and thumb of his right hand, which was maimed in 1978 by the chain of a Triumph motorcycle. It ends at the knuckle with a smooth, scarred lump. He smells like molded fruit, mint, and engine grease, and he could knock the teeth from a draft mule.

I was in the backyard with my cousin Charlie peeling the lid from one of Uncle Dale's old dip cans. The bullfrog we stuffed into it was reduced to a lump of bloated fat. Its pocked skin reflected the evening sun, ambient and exasperated. We dumped the frog onto the concrete patio and stared at it. I was waiting. Waiting for it to move, to hop out of the

Void and onto the fescue under Grandma's pecan tree. We could have waited forever. My tiny index finger caressed its belly, wishing it would twitch, kick, piss—*do something*.

Many such moments of senseless cruelty rest uncomfortably among my memories of boyhood. Childhood's wonder radiates once I've lifted myself from the guilt of those moments. Lying on a soft layer of dead leaves in the Cross Timbers of Oklahoma, staring past the tangle of blackjack limbs to the sky, watching the clouds race from the Great Plains as if startled by the rolling thunder to the west. My memories of wonder grow from such instances of placid chaos.

The protests at Standing Rock were shut down with bulldozers and militarized cops. I did my best to play the role of grad student. The slow onset of collapse can wear on you, and I embraced it with a non-intellectual sort of nihilism. I was feeling apathetic, black-pilled as they say, thinking the world was bound for flames, when I came across a bunch of folks marching and chanting against the treatment of water protectors near the Clark Fork River in downtown Missoula. It was deep into winter, January maybe. The nights are long then but they never get black. An inversion lurks over the lights of Missoula causing a purple haze to envelope the valley in winter. Never darkness. Only the glow of the town reflected onto itself. At night atop Lolo peak, you can see Missoula incandescent among the expanse. Like a musical note from the womb, it announces itself to the blackness of empty space. A testament to the isolation that Montana can allow.

Yael showed up late to the protest, muttering about work as she crawled from her old Ford pickup, dirty white with a bumper that had seen a collision or two. Her hair was short and disheveled. We ended up on either end of a long, waving banner with *Water is Life* scribed across the front. As I sat leaning my back against the red brick office of a Montana senator, I watched her draw pictures of mountains and sunshine on the back of a cardboard protest sign, entertaining a group of children that were crying with boredom. She was gruff, but she was perceptive and sensitive when she knew others were suffering.

She was brought to tears by a documentary about trophy hunting.

"I think you're an empath," I said.

"An empath? What's next, are you going to give me crystals to decalcify my pineal gland? Fuck off."

We walked to the riverside. We stood beside the flowing waters of the Clark Fork River, near the swell where the surfers hang out. The activists performed a water ceremony. There was a prayer in Lakota and an offering of tobacco.

Yael had loaded her truck with bikes and delivered them to Standing Rock. She met some organizers through her trip, and that landed her at the protest. A few of us piled into Yael's truck and drove to the Army Corp of Engineers office to gather information on the public comment period for the construction of the pipeline.

"Yeah, I just got out of a relationship. We're trying to split up the junk we collected together. You know, you're with somebody that long, five years, it gets hard to tell what's yours from what's theirs. I got stuck with this clunker." She slapped the dashboard, "He gave me some cash for our Subaru. I got the raw end of the deal, if you ask me. Watch this."

She turned the wheel, gave it some gas, and the truck fishtailed.

"Piece of shit doesn't get traction. Even with all the sandbags in the back. Didn't make any difference. They always say 'buy American, buy American.' Well, I ain't buying American again if this is the kinda rust bucket we're putting on the streets. I'm gonna sell it. Figure I can get a grand out of it. Maybe fifteen hundred if I'm lucky. Even then I'll feel a little bad for the poor fucker it gets dumped on. Hope they got more use for it than I do."

She told me about her work as a wildland firefighter, as a researcher following pika through the mountains of New

Mexico as they fled climate change, as a lab researcher studying avian bioacoustics, and a wilderness ranger spending night after night alone in grizzly country, armed only with bear spray because she could never bring herself to kill a large carnivore. If it was her or them, then it was her time to go. That's just how she felt about it.

I said Yael was gruff, but perhaps gruff is not an accurate description. Imagine sitting at the breakfast table on a quiet Sunday morning. It is late spring in Montana so the windows are propped open with old encyclopedias, letting in cool air and the smell of blooming lilacs when Yael says, "You give me a wooden baseball bat and five minutes alone with that piece-of-shit [energy CEO], and it'll be nothing but brain matter and splinters when I come out," as if she were commenting on the rich taste of her morning tea over a plate of humanely sourced eggs cooked over easy. And you get it, because the looming collapse and those perpetuating it wreck your day, every single day and you feel powerless in the face of it all so you want to destroy something and it might as well be the skull of one of these greedy bastards who have no conscience and are stripping the world of everything that is good and causing the whole fucking problem. You quickly sympathize, nodding your head, breathing in the smell of your coffee as it floats in union with the lilacs and the sound of the honey bees in the garden; you can barely glimpse the peaks of the Absaroka mountains and you decide that everything around you in that moment is what you want to live for and what you want to defend.

The bullfrog was trying to get away from us, kicking and urinating all over our hands. Grandma Owens told us that's how kids got warts. They played in frog piss. We didn't care. We were going to catch it, stuff it into an empty dip can, and have us a good time.

I didn't think we'd kill it. I didn't think anything of it, really. Figured we could harass this frog a bit then carry on with our night. It must have been the Fourth of July, because there were fireworks being shot off from the Air Force base creating big red, white, and blue explosions in the sky. Charlie's sister, Liz, who is younger than us, asked, "Why are y'all hurting that frog?"

"Go away, Liz!"

Liz told me she had a special connection with the hornets that built a nest on the back porch. The same nest Grandad always shot with his pellet gun. Liz believed she had an unspoken, psychic agreement with the hornets; she didn't shoot them with the lever action Daisy, and in exchange, they didn't sting her. She demonstrated this one afternoon when we got back from school. Liz walked over to the hornet's nest and let a big one crawl onto her finger. She held it out to show me with a smile so big I watched her uvula hanging from the back of her throat. But five seconds into the trick that hornet plunged its stinger so far into her finger that it coulda hit bone. Hell, it might have come out the other side. Her wide smile turned into a scream, and I could still see that uvula flapping around inside her throat. I laughed so hard I keeled over in the grass with my stomach feeling like a ball of rubber bands.

"That frog didn't do nothing to y'all. Leave it alone!"

"Shut up, Liz!"

Charlie walked over and punched her in the arm.

"I hate you, you jerk!" she screamed and ran inside.

We considered the Liz situation handled.

But the frog was still kicking, trying to keep its legs from being stuffed in the can. We sealed the lid, and the can continued to move around as the frog struggled inside.

It was late May when Yael and I dragged Kira, her sixty-pound lab mutt, toward an ancient juniper in Utah's Logan valley. Kira was shitting liquid from her flea and tick medication. A gray sky was letting out fierce thunder—a booming that echoed through the ponderosas, dripping from the pine needles and swallowing the silence. It made Kira anxious. For the past few weeks we'd been shooting my old .22 while stuffing her slobbering jowls with diced hotdogs, hoping she wouldn't tuck tail when we fired the 12-gauge on upland bird. Yael stroked her and said, "Don't worry, the thunder is just like a big gun shot."

We climbed higher past a trail crew cutting through fallen cedars. All of it was covered by a thin mist drifting upon the crest through a wheeling expanse of green trees and stone that heaved up and down, tempting the patience of the stratus clouds to the east. We trekked further, losing a bit of altitude, and I ran my hand over the long grass that lined the trail. When I saw that juniper, I thought of Jesus. It kind of looked like Jesus had he been a contortionist. The gnarled limbs pointed out east and west. Little organic explosions forming a green crown on its skyward spire.

The juniper was seeded some 1,500 years ago during the twilight of the Roman empire. A time when they and the Persians were, once again, spilling each other's guts. Soon the Roman empire succumbed to the universal feature of every great civilization: collapse. Centuries of blood had already soaked our primate skin. Human life thrived in vast graveyards, nurtured by the vital fluid of any wayward son-of-a-bitch who dared cross the line into our territory, sexual or otherwise.

Lightning cracked through the doughy starkness of the clouds. The dog flinched. Her ears fell back. Her eyes bounced untrusting inside her head. We tore apart a cheese stick and stuffed it into her mouth. They call this positive association. From now on, a loud boom means cheese, salami, hotdogs, so boom is good. No analysis needed.

We soon realized the downside of this. Hoping to alleviate her anxiety when crossing horses and mules, we introduced her to tame stock while stuffing her mouth with whatever greasy, fatty thing we had on hand. We succeeded. She had no fear of horses. Yet, the problem is obvious. A dog should fear a kicking horse.

Charlie and I tossed the thing around. First in the lawn a couple feet apart, then a few more feet and a few more until we were on opposite sides of the yard, backs rubbing against the fence. The disc hovered in the sky like a UFO carrying an alien laboratory where they test poor, unsuspecting frogs for the affliction of claustrophobia.

"Let's throw it over the fence. I'll go into the yard next door," Charlie said from across the lawn.

As he walked over, I kicked around pecans. Picked one up, tried to crack it between my teeth, failed, spit it out.

"Ok, here it comes!" he yelled.

I saw the black disc soaring through the sky. The frog was a subject in this senseless experiment at the hands of our brutal alien species. All of this was set into a sherbet-orange sky, wily and life-giving.

An esoteric dust swept across the slick rock as we rumbled south through Grand Staircase-Escalante. Tumbleweeds crawled across a leering red infinity that swallowed and bared itself to the heat of the swollen sun. The sweltering horizon was obscured, as if a translucent Jell-O was cooking upon the desert sand.

We were traveling back to Oklahoma for the wedding of two old friends. It was sure to be elegant. They have a taste for fine things. There would be music and dancing and food, drinks and laughter, and we'd talk about how much we missed each other, and then go on speaking once a year. There would be a transient grace to the whole affair. I've always been satisfied with grime and dust, sleeping comfortably on the soft bulge of the underbelly. Such concessions were necessary for a life of movement, though I am growing older and the thought of slowing down seems more colorful with every passing day.

We found a spot to park the car where the rock curved down toward our camp forming a dusty amphitheater, and we built a fire. Turkey vultures cut slits through the open sky, hinds afire, driven by the day's last chance for carrion. They swept up what was left of the light, trapping dusk in the white of their tail feathers. Kira collected piles of desiccated cow dung in her bed and food bowl. Unashamed, she masticated the hardened patties. Her lips curled away from her teeth in a sort of coerced joy, or maybe it was blissful remorse. I couldn't be sure.

Yael was slouched into a woven camp chair near the fire, her form only half revealing itself to the matrix of night. Twilight etched the curves of her lips and chin and the small dent that runs along the right side of her face where she was kicked by a quarter horse when she was nine years old. It moves when she talks or clenches her jaws. It comes right up to the corner of her eye—any closer and it would've popped out of the socket. A bottle of bourbon was stuffed between her thighs. She sneered at the dog. "You better stop eating shit Kira, or you're gonna get worms." She took a long pull from the bottle and wiped the dribble from her face with the back of her hand.

Kira looked at her with the flames of the fire spinning like Dervishes in her eyes, curious and defiant. She considered this warning for only a moment then plunged her newly grown canines into an old, gray cow patty.

In the morning, we walked. The echoes of the flies buzzed through the slot canyons. It was a ghostly chorus that made me think the voices of our ancestors were speaking to us through the fabric of time. The division between planes seems thinner in the desert. The desert is like New Orleans in that way. Even when civilization encroaches, the desert resists. We rested at a pool of water. Rippling red and blue, the lonely basin permeated like breath, or momentary awareness, beginning and ending in a vast expansion of being. Bright moss glistened on the rock, and Kira slid unwittingly into the water. She learned to swim.

I rested under a girth of sandstone hanging over the pool, protruding into sunlight and sparing me the oppression of

June's heat. Black desert varnish dripped down the rock face. That black varnish is a significant mystery, puzzled over for decades by Darwin and leagues of scientists. Made up of clay, iron, and manganese, its layers hold history, like the rings of timeworn trees. Throughout the region petroglyphs are etched into varnish-covered stone depicting people, animals, and odd, otherworldly forms that gave rise to theories of extraterrestrial contact.

Riding the ripples of the pool were the teardrop leaves that fell from the cottonwoods fluttering above. They signal water for travelers of the arid Southwest. A representation of the doggedness of life, like weeds through cracked concrete or the matsutake mushrooms that grew from the desolation of Hiroshima. The fluffy seeds of the cottonwood floated overhead, little souls in transit.

As Kira played, silt rose from the bottom of the pool. Through the haze I saw tiny apparitions—startled tadpoles fleeing her revelry. Yael laughed, splashing water into the air that Kira leapt at, catching it in her mouth. Pushed forward by the momentum of her joy, Kira crashed feet first into a silver cholla cactus, which left its fine needles planted between the pads of her feet. Startled by the sudden shift from bliss to agony, she plopped down, put her ears back, and stuffed her snout into the white, butterfly shape in the middle of her chest. Yael and I spent fifteen minutes holding her still and pulling the cactus needles from her feet. Kira gyrated wildly, kicking Yael in the face and chest as I pulled the needles free. Kira never recovered the blissful jaunt that she'd carried through the water. She lay down, stubborn and unmoving, so we took turns carrying her through the midday heat two miles back to the car.

Later, as we stood on the edge of Goblin Valley, the sunset melted across the vista like a stick of illuminated butter on the sands of the West. The shadows of the hoodoos stretched, elongating across the desert. They grew long with the passage of time, until they became thin like a razor's edge. Then the moment was gone before I ever knew it happened.

Many boys seem to be stewed in meanness. Like there is a projector shining onto the inside of our mother's swollen stomach that displayed images of cruelty, and it's all we see until the moment we're brought into the world. I've been at odds with the corruption of boyhood, not childhood, but boyhood, those moments of youth that seem to be born from an intrinsic brutality. Charlie and I stuffed that frog into Uncle Dale's empty chew can and tossed it around like a Frisbee. We threw it back and forth over the cedar fence, and somewhere in the back of my mind, I knew that the act was cruel, senseless. I pushed those feelings down and indulged in a boorish glee that felt almost instinctive. Yet, once it was there, distended and oblong, my detachment materialized before me, and I was struck by my first glance at the outcome of that willful violence. The frog was dead, and it was dead because of me.

Wilderness, like that barren desert expanding all around me, doesn't demonize or reward this behavior. There is brutality there. But it calls for community as well as fierce independence. It is a space where we feel both alone and interconnected. A mirror of the coming and going that constitutes being. We are at our most vulnerable and our most secure. Wonder peers through anger and carnage, and all that chaos merges into a single thread.

Kira got worms. In the distance, the La Sals rose from a collapsed panorama as astral titans, their peaks bearing no sign of winter, already dehydrated after a dry season. The place was crawling with ATVs. The endless *weeee!* of two-stroke engines had me convinced we were passing through the creaking gates of Hell, but we had no choice. Welcome to Moab.

Outdoor gear shops and New Age boutiques lined the streets, and everything was glowing with the artificial vibrancy of high season in a tourist town. We checked into a cheap motel and hunkered down until the vet appointment the next morning. I grabbed a beer and hit the hot tub. The warm water bubbled around me. I avoided the jets, because they make my skin itch. Neon lights gave the water an otherworldly glow, mimicking the bioluminescence of jellyfish and certain algae. I stretched out, letting the cool breeze make the wet hair on my arms stand straight.

The next morning, after Kira's vet appointment, we took a short hike out to Corona arch, near the train tracks that once carried all the uranium mined after the nuclear weapons boom that followed WWII and the creation of the Atomic Energy Act. This legislation ensured that the US government was the only entity buying and selling uranium. With dynamite, they carved out large canyons into the slick rock and laid their train tracks. We hopped along the railroad ties and looked up to the blue sky which was thin and perpendicular between the high walls blasted into the landscape.

Kira's young pads were too soft for the heat of the sand, so we got little leather slippers to tie around her ankles. The arch exploded from the flat top of a mesa, curving into the stark lip of slick rock below. We ate dried bananas in the arch's shadow. I watched three young boys chase a zebra-tailed lizard around a cliffrose shrub. An older man, who appeared to be the father of one of the boys, sat facing the other direction with his eyes locked on his phone. Beside him was a young girl with wild blonde curls falling from her head. She asked the man if she could pet Kira. He said no. The boys bellowed as the lizard juked and circled around, burrowing itself in the tangle of the cliffrose.

"You run around the other side of the bush, scare it, and I'll grab it."

"Then what?"

"Then I'll throw it off the cliff!"

In my mind, I saw the bullfrog rotting on the porch in Grandma Owens's backyard, still wet and bloated, cooking into the cement. It is not the transgression itself that bothers me. It was just a frog, yes, but frogs are, famously, an indicator species, so I am left again thinking about the cruelty in boyhood. If it is not universal, it is devastatingly prevalent, from drum fish to bullfrogs. And that cruelty carries on through boyhood into old men who don uniforms and hold office. Our critiques of so-called *toxic masculinity* feel shortsighted. It's a critique that has been so abstracted that it is hard to define, but our instinctive brutality is a deeply corrupting force that causes a rift between a man and his soul. This problem is not self-contained, it spills out into our society in the form of suicides, rapes, and mass shootings. The top of the world is the hardest place from which to fall. The world wants to leave the ideologies of traditional masculinity behind and men don't know how to cope with that.

The challenge for the modern kid who feels compelled to adhere to the archetypes of traditional masculinity then seems to be the pursuit of a *detoxification*, a maintaining of an ethical ruggedness without the entitlement, the pretension, the unfounded anger and cruelty of traditional masculinity. My buddy Murray once said he fears the passing of Willie Nelson. For him, Willie represents the last model for a ruggedness that is also defined by kindness, care, and sensitivity. As if to cite a source and solidify his point Murray turned on Willie's version of "Cowboys Are Frequently, Secretly Fond of Each Other" as we sat in my truck hiding from a sudden rain that overtook the Big Hole Wilderness.

For the past five years, I have worked tirelessly to re-establish, or rather re-recognize, the intimate relationship between myself and the mesh of life constituted by atom, being, ecosystem, Earth, universe, ad infinitum, upward or downward, inward and out. For that, I have a laundry list of things to thank: books, conversation, psychedelics, travel, isolation, lovers, community, music, a backpack and a pair of boots, because within the empty grip of the wild, gender is lost. It is an ongoing struggle, and we're nowhere close to figuring out, but a hard truth is better than a soft lie.

After we left the arch, the pallid bats swooped through our camp, swallowing the mosquitos that buzzed despite the smoke of juniper and pinyon pine rising from our fire. In a few days my feet would touch the red dirt of Oklahoma's mud rather than Utah's slick rock or Montana's mountains. I could see it already, those oil rigs nodding like heads, the monocrops spreading below the spinning blades of windmills, all of it feeding homes and bellies inside America's great chorus of consumption.

THE GENERATIONS
FORGET EACH OTHER

———————————

The monarchs were drifting through a drought in early fall, over parched grass—delicate, yellowed needles. One of these travelers landed on my finger in my parents' backyard, lightly waving its orange and black wings like opaque stained-glass windows. This butterfly was likely of the sixth generation to be born on its migration. A never-ending trip across America, pit stops for death and rebirth, check points of reincarnation, grueling, moving forward toward nothing certain for the sake of flux. Their grand scheme only a patterned chaos. Their purpose—being. Their tendencies wrapped in aimlessness.

Edward Lorenz—mathematician, meteorologist, and pioneer of chaos theory—popularized the term *butterfly effect*. The idea that the world's phenomena can be attributed to something brings comfort to many. But what good is knowing there is always a cause if you can't foresee the reaction? We love an explanation but can't bear to ponder consequences. Though Lorenz coined the term, the idea that we can alter the immense entirety of things by moving a single grain of sand was posited long before by Johann Gottieb Fichte in his book *The Vocation of Man*. Indeed, philosophy has always been better at getting to the top of things than getting to the bottom of them. Our misguided decisions that echo through generations, rather than being stuck in time, are stuck *to* time.

The monarch shuffled its legs and moved up my wrist, flapping its wings lethargically, and I got swept up in an illusion. Time slowed down. I imagined a grandfather clock tipped over across my mind. The seconds moved like minutes. Even the breeze seemed like a slow exhalation. The monarch lifted its wings until they came together, pointing toward a sky empty but for a few pale clouds. The green grass of the lawn blurred in the background, a manufactured landscape set aside so I could focus for a precious few seconds on this butterfly. The seconds like minutes.

It moved its wings down and I saw my grandmother as a child coughing up the dirt of a dust storm on the plains eighty years ago. It moved its wings up and I saw the tornado that chewed through her house twenty years ago. It moved its wings down and I saw a deep injection well and a tectonic shift and an earthquake five years ago. Wings up, the polar vortex moves south, wings down the ocean acidifies, wings up the methane clathrate released from permafrost. Wings up. Wings down. Another second, another tragedy. The seconds like minutes.

The monarch's ever-moving population has declined for a number of reasons. One of these is the increase in illegal deforestation in Mexico. In the town of Cherán, the people violently resisted illegal logging and the armed guards of the cartel that protected those operations. The people of Cherán, in Michoacán state, mostly Indigenous and disenfranchised, armed themselves and resisted those mechanisms of economic and environmental devastation. After going through their own transformation from survivors of corrupt government and resource extraction to militant agitators, the Indigenous Purepecha people drove out the cartels, the government officials, and the loggers. Government on every level failed the people of Cherán. These were ancestral forests being cut down; the deforestation was a desecration of the sacred. They asked repeatedly for assistance, but their cries for help went unheeded. Now they are an autonomous, self-governing city of 20,000 people, 16,000 of whom are Indigenous.

While half of America was aghast after Trump's election, a large number of Indigenous peoples, many of whom were freezing in South Dakota protesting the construction of the Dakota Access pipeline, seemed unmoved. The tribes have endured violent subjugation at the hands of every single American president: the unacknowledged history of genocide and colonization, the doomed relocation programs, the imposed conditions on the reservations, the systematic erasure of culture and religion.

The monarchs inherit their understanding of life. They know which direction to migrate and where to overwinter because they are biologically guided toward that place, and the landscape has always validated those biological inclinations. The monarch's patterned history is written into their genetics. The Indigenous people of this country have inherited the trauma of genocide passed on through genes and generations of storytellers. The atrocities echo through time, permeating from the soil below my feet as the monarch postured itself above my wrist, soon to be pushed forward, driven by unseen forces that are as much a part of this planet as Oklahoma's red dirt.

Friedrich Nietzsche's idea of eternal recurrence suggests that we should live our lives as if we are going to have to live them over and over again, like monarchs migrating across the belly of America. Like Lorenz, Nietzsche wasn't the first to posit this theory. It was espoused by ancient Indian religions and adopted by the Pythagoreans and the Stoics. The universe expands and contracts in a way that we will do everything we do infinitely. From the big bang, the molecular sprawl expands into the Void until it can stretch no more. Somewhere along the way, planet Earth whirls into a brief existence that's both miraculous and catastrophic. Then it flickers into non-being and waits until the universe implodes upon the fragility of its cosmic stretch.

In *The Unbearable Lightness of Being*, Milan Kundera suggests the opposite. Everything we do, we do only for one fleeting moment as we ride the gust of a unique universal breath. The conclusion is the same: whatever we do we should do with passion and caring, either because we're going to do it again and again, or because we can do it only once.

But then how can I bear it when I hear of children whose brief lives were defined most starkly by suffering only to then be taken away by bombs or genocide or starvation? Or the countless species that have been driven extinct by the recklessness of our civilization? America's history is carried on the shoulders of subsequent generations who bear the psychic weight of our endless brutality. Will they bear it only once before perishing into the finality of non-being, or will they relive their suffering endlessly?

The butterfly moved its legs, ending the illusion of time inching by. It crawled over my knuckles. I slowly squeezed my hand closed, watching it travel over them, up and down, like the Wichitas that rise from southern Oklahoma. Ancient hills that were once great mountains, the Indigenous tribes of the plains consider them to be holy places fit for noble tales and wondrous ceremonies. N. Scott Momaday's titular *Rainy Mountain* is housed within those rolling hills. They rest modestly upon the flat horizon like aging harlots crooking their legs into the skyline for anyone who'll look. Those hills have hidden Cherokee outlaws, no longer indentured to the flagrant graces of genocidal governments big and small.

The butterfly made it to the end of my pinky and stopped as if to contemplate the edge. Of what concern is a fall if you can fly, I wonder. Perhaps this is the logic that gets us thinking we can invent our way out of ecocide and extinction. Visions of space colonies, fully automated factories, carbon sponges, robot bees, and atmospheric shades that block the heat of the sun.

Herbicides used on monocrop operations across the state

of Oklahoma and the Midwest have wiped out nearly 60% of the milkweed flora in the region. The monarchs co-evolved with the milkweed and the wildflowers that provide the nectar to fatten them up for their long journey to Mexico. The fourth generation of monarchs on the yearly migration is born from the milkweed. The leaves serve as a roost for incubating the eggs until they are ready to hatch. The destruction of the milkweed leaves the monarchs to fly lost, looking for yet another home consumed by human development.

I lifted my eyes from the monarch, and I looked at the old tree house my father built for my sister and me when we were children. It hasn't been used in a decade or more. There are fewer kids at my folks' place now than there used to be. Even fewer kids who want to climb the creaking ladder into that rickety old thing. Swings hang from it. They move only with the wind now. The wind can get so strong it pushes them back and forth as if ghosts have risen up from the plains to ride the swings into the sky, up and down, toward those thin clouds, pale and meandering.

Oklahoma was Indian Country before the land run. It was seen as valueless desolation before they discovered all that oil beneath the red dirt. It was known as the Unassigned Lands that marked the end of the Trail of Tears, a brutally enforced migration across America. Then in the late 1800's they opened the land to white settlers. The Indigenous population was isolated one last time to small sections of the state designated as reservations, and the final step was taken to separate the tribes from their ancestral lands. How many times will the Cherokee, the Creek, the Chickasaw, the Seminole make this doomed migration?

In Oklahoma, we still celebrate the land run. We re-enact it as grade schoolers, building our wagons and staking our claims. The University's mascot is the Sooner; those who cheated during the land run and laid claim to the land early. Land that was then twice stolen.

I sat once in a butterfly garden in China. It was a dome-shaped greenhouse with candelabra primrose, azaleas, and rhododendrons. I watched children slapping the butterflies to the ground, stomping them with their feet and laughing. My Mandarin was no good, but even if it had been, I wouldn't have said anything. Still, I couldn't sit there and watch, so I left. I bought watermelon from a farmer on the side of a dirt road. I ate it and let its sweetness wash over my senses. It was the best watermelon I'd ever tasted. I watched a truck drive by with a group of dust-covered Buddhists monks being tossed around in the bed, and the children went on gleefully killing. I just wasn't watching.

Zhangzi wanted to know, after awakening from a dream of being a butterfly, if he was a man dreaming of being a butterfly or a butterfly dreaming of being a man. Maybe it's both. Our biological subconscious pushes forward the history of suffering and brutality as well as privilege and luxury. The mess goes unseen as we bear witness to the trauma of a dying planet. All of us, the rich assholes and the poor assholes.

I sometimes have dreams too. A bright sun reveals itself to the grasslands through a haze. It watches for centuries as pride swallows our civilization and our history. It smiles as our broken planet once again looks as it should. The butterflies pour from my stomach and follow the milkweed back to Michoacán. The scars of humanity exist for a brief period, only a moment inside the breath of the universe. There are organisms, ecosystems hoping to help us in our moment of frailty, so we can be reborn, transformed in the vision of the wild. Yet the new us always looks an awful lot like the old us. Latching onto our previous incarnations, there's no progress, only static regression. I don't mourn our loss. I mourn the loss of what we could have been.

The life of the butterfly is defined by movement, rebirth, revolution. The monarch has seen the comings and goings of eons, the passing of species, the devastation of asteroids, but nothing so foolhardy and destructive as human ingenuity and the progress of civilization. They suffer through the purification of the monocrop fields by Monsanto's pesticides. Through the harvesting of ancient forests that have marked the beginning and the end of their ceaseless journey. After 175 million years of coming and going in a cycle like breath, they are being annihilated.

It lifted itself from my finger and drifted away toward the top of a magnolia tree. There were still a couple of flowers blooming. The white vortexes holding time—flora swirling in futures and pasts. The butterfly landed on the blossom for a moment before it carried on to go and die in Texas. No one wants to die in Texas. But so it is.

For us, this place will never look as it is meant to. The glory of wildness is now isolated to pockets of government-enforced preserves, the path of the butterflies interrupted. If the flap of a butterfly's wings can cause a hurricane, then what are we doing with our mining, our monocrops, our drilling, our methane? And if the abuse we subject others to, human and more than human, can be carried through time on an epigenetic wave, then how long will the consequences of these actions echo?

The butterfly will move on toward uncertainty. The generations die only to have pushed the roost forward. Do those that reach the golden land know that they have made it? Do they appreciate the rest, or do they wish they had seen Oklahoma? When the woods are gone will they keep traveling south and find a beach in Honduras? Or will they rest in the expanse of the clear cuts, exhausted and bathing in defeat? Perhaps the next generation won't know any better. They never saw the forests of Michoacán.

I used to see great big groups of Monarchs flying through the air, resting on the grayish bark of oaks. I watched one flapping in slow, pained movements, lifting itself up and down on the windowsill, crushed from a collision with the glass. It reminded me of wrestling as a child. When I was on my back and going to be pinned, I struggled frantically, trying to lift my shoulders from the mat so I wouldn't be defeated. The monarch kept lifting itself, up and down, up and down for the final agonizing moments of its life. I watched for a number of minutes. Up and down. Up and down. I felt little. I didn't understand why.

EPILOGUE

North America's only marsupial, a critter that can be found flattened, entrails baking into steaming asphalt, or stiff and salivating with teeth bared and anal glands leaking: the noble possum. Freshly killed, the possum can be used in a number of savory recipes including, but not limited to, stuffed possum, possum and sweet potatoes, possum chili, and possum pot pie. Its taste has been praised by such honorable Americans as Mark Twain, Jimmy Carter, and my Great Uncle Jed. Possum grease (or possum oil) can be used as a chest rub and an arthritic remedy, due to its richness in essential fatty acids. The moral being, don't let good roadkill go to waste.

Funny thing possums do, they abduct stray cats and bestow upon them their fighting style. I imagine there's nothing more streetwise and scrappy than a possum-trained tom. Rough-and-tumble bunch those old possums, solitary drifters, finding home in a world of destitution, like old folk singers.

Possums are able to shake off rattlesnake bites no problem due to peptides that neutralize the snake venom. The Sioux have a prophecy of the devastation brought about by a black snake, *Zuzeca Sape*. It was understood as a warning against the Dakota Access Pipeline, or a larger prophecy concerning the construction of pipelines over sacred and wild lands.

Oklahoma is a Choctaw phrase, originally *okla humma*,

which can be translated to red people. Possum, on the other hand, is Powhatan for white dog. Yes, Oklahoma is a land of white dogs and red people, white trash and rednecks, white nationalists and red communists. I rather think that the possum stands as a fair representation of many Okie folk. A good number of us having grown immune, fighting off the infiltration of black snakes. Too often considered a rodent, flattened by the reality of *progress*, not always easy to stomach, but forever resilient. Selling our souls and our bodies, we live off the scraps of civilization.

Sometimes the winds of the plains are the only thing to break the infinite silence. They come in cockeyed, making oak leaves speak to my flesh, expanding my sense of self beyond me. I look at the geometry of the night sky and wonder how many times my mind has been sculpted from red dirt, how many times a child has blown the same red dirt from her cast iron cornbread mold, how many times a red dirt-covered car has run out of gas in Buckeye, Arizona, within the endless undulation of the universe?

Many believe that we can inherit the trauma of the past, carrying with us the crimes committed against and by our ancestors. I can buy that: consciousness gestated in a pool of black amniotic oil. When I slow down, I catch residual glimpses of that void. I wonder what would happen if people felt that, you know, really understood the vitality of what we're protecting and the fracture we can cause in the shared psyche of future generations.

When the seasons change in Talimena State Park, a rolling expanse of red and yellow crosses the state line into Arkansas. Soon it'll be a sea of black bones, the oaks and elms and dogwoods having retired into their plane of rest. As for me, I have no time for rest. I'm merely playing possum. Lying stiff with kin threatened by the vehicle of industry, sustained by vice and chewing through the fuel of wilderness. Certainly, some of us have been caught up in the cyclone of the spinning wheels, mangled by the mechanisms of modernity, but the dead speak a language of prophecy, whispering across time into our cosmic blueprint.

ACKNOWLEDGMENTS

First, thanks to Nate Perkins for the time and the vision. Please judge this book by its cover because Rachel Pfeffer killed it. All the people who read it and made it hive mind instead of my mind: Goldie, Fiji, Lo, Big Bear, Anna, Erica, other Mason (the one with less chaos in his eyes), Patrick, JD, and Scooter. Who am I missing?

All the teachers: Susan Kates, Jonathan Stalling, Louis Economides, Teresa Wilkerson, Catherine John, Katie Kane, and Geary Hobson.

Amy and Danny and their Boheme Apotheca in Livingston. Occult book club kept it weird and gave me fuel during the writing process.

Richard Manning who made me ask hard questions. Robert Michael Pyle who pushed me closer to the high ridge of the mind. Phil Condon who convinced me it was real.

Shy for letting them know.

Steven Arcieri for helping me carve the word from the sentence.

The De(Generate) crew.

Any and all lit mags that have published me. Stu at *Bear Creek Gazette* for paying me. Rhyd at *Gods & Radicals* for paying me too.

Wind through the window in early summer. The great horned owl over the Musselshell River. The snow on Lolo peak come late spring.

Thanks to my mom, my dad, my sister, and my family for just rolling with it. Whatever it is. I love you for it.

Thanks to Becca for reading this maybe more than I did. For wanting to see the world and dragging me along. For being the best manifestation of the good this place has to offer. I get the happiness thing now.

It's better.

Mason Parker is an Okie-born, Montana-based writer. He holds an MS in Environmental Studies from the University of Montana. His work has been featured in *X-R-A-Y*, *Hobart*, the *International Journal of Wilderness*, and *BULL Men's Fiction*. In his free time he enjoys exploring the Selway-Bitterroot Wilderness with his partner and two dogs.

OTHER VERY FINE TITLES FROM
TRIDENT PRESS

Blood-Soaked Buddha/Hard Earth Pascal
by Noah Cicero

it gets cold
by jasper avery

Major Diamonds Nights & Knives
by Katie Foster

Cactus
by Nathaniel Kennon Perkins

The Pocket Emma Goldman

Sixty Tattoos I Secretly Gave Myself at Work
by Tanner Ballengee

The Pocket Peter Kropotkin

The Silence is the Noise
by Bart Schaneman

The Pocket Aleister Crowley

Propaganda of the Deed:
The Pocket Alexander Berkman

Los Espiritus
by Josh Hyde

The Soul of Man Under Socialism
by Oscar Wilde

www.tridentcafe.com/trident-press-titles

9 781951 226145